The Last Circuit Preacher

Loran Hugh Parker

Note for Librarians: A cataloguing record for this book is available from Library
and Archives Canada at www.collectionscanada.ca/amicus/index-e.html

Printed in Victoria, BC, Canada.

ISBN: 978-1-4269-1366-2 (Soft)
ISBN: 978-1-4269-1367-9 (Hard)

Library of Congress Control Number: 2009931995

 www.trafford.com

North America & international
toll-free: 1 888 232 4444 (USA & Canada)
phone: 250 383 6864 ♦ fax: 812 355 4082 ♦ email: info@trafford.com

To our son and family minister for more than 25 years,
Douglas Keith Parker–
May your ministry always be fulfilling,
and your life dedicated to God's service.

And to our daughter,
Pamela June Nelson–
May you always remain faithful
to your church, your family, and your friends.

INTRODUCTION

The Last Circuit Preacher is a historical, creative nonfiction book about the life and times of my father, Benjamin Franklin (Ben) Parker Jr. Throughout his entire adult lifetime, he was a farmer and part-time preacher. During his earlier years, he was a layman in the Methodist church in Texas, and preached only when his pastor was away. A move to Oklahoma and the devastating effects of the Great Depression caused him to lose his minister's license and steer away from preaching. However, during the last eight years of his life, from 1940 to 1948, he was a circuit preacher to a group of small churches in south-central Oklahoma.

The Last Circuit Preacher contains nostalgia, family values, history and Americana in abundance. It describes a way of life long since lost, and now forgotten. It describes a time when a man's word was as binding as any contract—a time when you could count on your fellow man to do the right thing—a time when your neighbor would help you if you needed it.

The Last Circuit Preacher is a story that needs to be told. And, who best to tell it but one who was close to this man and observed his life on a daily basis. This book chronicles the life of a man of integrity, honesty, and impeccable moral values: one worthy of being emulated. Although he didn't see himself as such, Ben Parker was a real-life hero to many of his peers.

SOME THINGS YOU NEED TO KNOW

I am not a historian. I am a storyteller. A historian is duty-bound to report the facts accurately and completely. A storyteller is not bound by such strict guidelines.

I am also an incurable romantic. I relish the events of the past which affect my life; those experienced by me and those told to me by my siblings. I recall in vivid detail many of the events which tell my father's story.

The events described in this book are true, if by "true" you mean the events actually happened. However, there's no way I can remember the exact words spoken by the characters in *The Last Circuit Preacher*. That's the reason I used the creative nonfiction genre. I do, however, remember in minute detail most of the events as they occurred. When my memory was vague on some historical facts, I researched to find what actually happened.

FORWARD

In *The Last Circuit Preacher*, Loran Parker captures the essence of a man deeply influenced by his faith in God. Ben Parker is the last circuit preacher who walks through the times and lives of his fellow man, portraying a man who faces the challenges of the historical Dust Bowl period and the deep Depression with a straightforward, strong determination to survive and to do so with grace and dignity. Throughout the story, time and again, he uses the opportunity to demonstrate his belief that "All things work together for good for those who love God and are called according to His purpose." Ben's legacy of a man of deep character and spiritual conviction resonates through the generations mentoring others by the revelation of his personal experiences. His descendants, as well as others who read his story, are left with appreciation, awe, admiration, and the knowledge that Ben's constant belief in the goodness of God governed every thought.

Loran recreates the story of Ben Parker through family lore and legend, personal heirloom documents and letters, and through historical research. The writing process of using creative nonfiction emphasizes the truth of his findings revealed in an entertaining and engaging manner with characterization, dialogue, and setting.

The result is a compelling story that leaves a reader with insight into a historical period of time as well as inspiration in the inherent goodness of man.

It has been my privilege in the last two years to follow the course of this work and watch it unfold each week. The diligence and perseverance of Loran's search to define Ben Parker is one of integrity and brings honor to his ancestry.

Janice Stevens
Instructor
Clovis Adult Education

TABLE OF CONTENTS

THE CALL

Ben almost always had devotions and Bible study in a spare stall in the barn.

"Oh, No! Please God. Not my little girl. She's only 13. Take me. I'm 53, and ready to go."

Ben was pleading with God about his daughter, Lavada. She was lying on the bed in the next room, with fever and chills, struggling to breathe. She had pneumonia and was not doing well.

Dr. Monroe had just left. "There's nothing I can do," he said. "Keep her comfortable. That's all I can tell you."

Ben's mind flashed back ten years to the time Lavada was three years old. She had diphtheria at that time and was not expected to live. Her temperature hovered around 105 degrees for three days. Dr. Monroe didn't give her any hope of surviving then either. She did survive, but the extremely high fever caused severe brain damage. Now she was again struggling for her life.

Lavada was growing into a lovely young lady. She was an exceedingly loving person, with childlike faith and trust in everyone. After her first illness, she had to learn everything over again. She never progressed beyond the skills and social graces of a five-year-old, but she dearly loved all the members of her family. Ben had a special love for Lavada, and would gladly give up his life for her.

Ben's thoughts returned to the present. Unless God performed a miracle, his little girl would surely die. He prayed, "God, I know You don't make mistakes. If it's Your will, would You please heal my little girl? If not, I am ready to accept Your decision."

Even though Ben's health was also failing, he sat up with Lavada all night, with the kerosene lamp burning. He watched her every movement and agonized over her labored breathing. The least he could do was be with her to the end.

The next morning, on Sunday, February 4, 1940, at 9:00, Lavada passed from this life to her heavenly home. Her struggles were over, but Ben was devastated, as were the other members of his family.

"You've been up all night. Why don't you get some sleep?" suggested Ben's wife, Tildie. "Loran and I will do the chores. Theta, would you wash the dishes? It would help me a lot."

"Yes, I will," answered five-year-old Theta.

"I'll get some sleep," Ben said. "I'm very tired."

Tildie and nine-year-old Loran went to the barn to milk the cows and feed the livestock. The rest of the farm labor would have to wait for a few days, until the present crisis was over.

Even though most people didn't have a telephone, news spread rapidly in rural Oklahoma. By late afternoon, almost all of Ben's neighbors had already heard of the passing of his little girl. They arranged a wake for her, to be held that night. The little two-room house where he and his family lived was filled with concerned neighbors, friends and relatives. Everyone comforted Ben and his family and showed their love in various ways.

The next morning, Ben and Tildie's oldest son, Francis, took him to Lindsay, to pick out a casket and arrange for the funeral. Embalming was seldom done in those days, so the burial was set for February 6, the next day. The Lindsay Funeral Home picked up Lavada's body that afternoon and got her ready for the services and the graveside rites.

After the funeral, most of the friends and family who attended returned to Ben and Tildie's house for a dinner, prepared by Tildie and some of her daughters and daughters-in-law. All of them pitched in and helped with the cooking.

During the dinner, many of Ben's relatives and friends offered comfort. "I feel your loss," Ben and Tildie's daughter, Gertrude, said. "I know it's not the same, but I loved her too. I'll miss her very much."

"She was such a sweet child," Gertrude's husband, Orville, said. "I know you'll miss her, but God can comfort you in your grief. He is faithful to His children."

Ben nodded in agreement, but said nothing. To talk at that time would most likely bring another flood of tears. He just didn't have anything to say at the time. Maybe later he could discuss his extreme grief, but not now.

Their company left after dinner and Ben was once again alone and sad. His thoughts returned to his little girl. He and Tildie had tried to give her an education, but she was not capable of learning all that the other children did. At the Oak Grove School, their daughter, Evelyn, guided Lavada and helped her as much as she could. When the family moved to the Pikes Peak School District, Loran took her under his wing. He befriended her and helped her learn as much as she was capable of grasping. The prior year, when Lavada was 12, the Pikes Peak School superintendent had Ben and Tildie in for a conference.

"Mr. and Mrs. Parker," he began. "Lavada has reached the limit of her abilities as far as school is concerned. By law, she can't be taken out of school until she has passed the eighth grade, or is 16 years old, but under the circumstances, I think we can get a waver for those requirements. I recommend she be dismissed from any further schooling."

Ben thought of these happenings and tears welled up in his eyes. He headed for the barn. It contained an extra stall where calves were sometimes housed in extremely cold weather. It was his prayer closet, the place where he met with God in prayer.

For the next several days, Ben was often seen going to the barn. His family knew he was going there for his prayer time, so they didn't bother him until he came out. Even so, one or more of the family would frequently hear him calling out to his Lord.

"God, I don't understand why my little girl was taken from me," they repeatedly heard him say, as tears streamed down his face. "She was such a joy to me, and it was my pleasure to have her home full time for the past year. I miss her so much."

One day, while in earnest prayer, Ben was silent for a few minutes. That's when he heard the voice. It was an almost audible sound inside his head. Ben immediately recognized it as God talking to him.

"Ben," the voice said. "I know you love your little girl very much. I know you want to die and be in heaven with her. I am aware of all your thoughts, but I have work for you to do for Me. I want you to return to ministering My gospel. When I am through with you, I will call you home and you can again be with Lavada. In the meantime, I will take good care of her. She will be in My hands."

Ben's mind returned to the time he was ministering as a layman in the Methodist church at Brock, Texas. He held that position for many years. Preaching the gospel was nothing new to him, but somehow he felt it would be different this time. He pondered the calling he had just received.

"As You wish," Ben answered. "If that's what You want, I am willing to be Your servant."

THE PONY RIDE

Ben's pony always came when he called

"Poppa, can I ride over to Jim Kellogg's house and go horseback riding with him?" Ben asked his father.

Even though the call back into the ministry ushered in a new phase in Ben's life, his existence began at his birth on September 29, 1886. His childhood was quite normal for the times but some events happened during his youth that helped to shape him into the loving, caring person he became.

None of Ben's family ever saw him ride a horse. It wasn't because he was afraid of them. He owned horses and mules his entire adult lifetime. He plowed with horses almost every day of his life. He hitched them to wagons and buggies, to take trips or to go into town.

Some members of his family reasoned that he was bucked off a horse, so was afraid to ride them. That probably isn't the case. Knowing him as I did, if he had been bucked off, he would have gotten back on and continued riding. Someone he was close to must have had a traumatic experience with horses, causing Ben to make a conscious decision never to ride a horse again.

It probably wasn't a member of Ben's family. If it had been, someone in the family would have known about it, but no such stories have surfaced.

Nobody will ever know the exact reason why he never rode a horse. Any explanation would be speculation. However, it could have happened as depicted in "The Pony Ride."

The date was Saturday, September 29, 1894. It was Ben's birthday, and he had turned eight that day. He didn't have to go to school, and he wanted to spend some time with his best friend.

Doc Parker thought about Ben's question. Doc really didn't need him at the store that day. He had finished his school lessons the night before, and his chores were done. What would it hurt to let him go?

"Sure," answered Doc. "I'll help you saddle Jericho. Just don't be out too late."

Ben followed Doc to the barn. Opening the gate to the pasture, Ben called, "Here, Jericho." His pony came galloping to him. He always came when he was called. Ben almost always had some treat for Jericho in his pocket, and he was anxious to see what it was.

Together, Ben and Doc began putting the saddle on Jericho. He was a gentle pony, nine years old and diminutive compared to Doc's other horses. He had passed him down to Ben when Ed outgrew him.

While they were saddling Jericho, Ben asked, "Poppa, why does everyone call you Doc? I know your name is Benjamin Franklin Parker because I'm named after you. Where did the name Doc come from?"

"It's a nickname," Doc answered. "Back in Alabama, during the Civil War, I was the oldest boy in our neighborhood. I was the only one big enough to doctor the livestock when they became ill. I doctored them for most of the folks in our area. Some of the ladies got to calling me Doc, and the name stuck. Many people around here don't even know what my real name is. They know me only as Doc."

"So, that's it," replied Ben. "I've been wondering, and John asked me in school the other day why you are called Doc."

The saddling was finished, and Ben led Jericho out of the barn. "Be careful," Doc called out, as his son mounted and rode off, kicking up dust as he left.

About a minute later, Ben left the small town of Brock, Texas and galloped along the country road. It was two miles to where his friend lived. That would give him about 15 minutes to just relax in the saddle and enjoy the countryside. The oak trees were beginning to show some of their fall color. There had been frost that morning, but it had melted off. Even so, there was a nip in the air as Ben rode Jericho along the dusty lane. It would be a good day for horseback riding. The horses would not tire as easily and the ride would be invigorating. He was looking forward to a ride with his special buddy.

Ben galloped up to the Kellogg's yard, reigned Jericho to a halt and called out, "Hey, Jim. Are you home?"

Jim came to the door. "I was hoping you would come over today," he answered. "How about a nice ride in the cool, fresh air?"

"That's what I came for."

"Let me get Ringo saddled. Have you had breakfast yet?"

"Yes, I ate early this morning. How about you?"

"I ate about an hour ago. Maybe I can get Mama to fix us a lunch. That way, we won't have to come home for dinner."

Jim went into the house and spoke briefly with his mother, then headed to the barn. While he saddled Ringo, Ben watched. "You remember John asking me why Poppa is called Doc?" he asked. "I found out this morning. It's a nickname given to him as a youngster."

"Did he doctor someone?" Jim asked.

"No. He doctored livestock during the Civil War. His neighbors called him Doc, and it stuck."

Jim finished saddling Ringo and led him to where Jericho was tied. He went into the house and returned with a cloth bag that contained two sandwiches and two cookies. "This will be enough for our dinner, won't it?" he asked.

"Sure will," Ben responded. "Are you ready to go?"

"Ready," Jim said.

The two boys mounted their ponies and headed toward the creek. It was one of their favorite places. They planned to ride along the water, gaze at the trees in their beautiful fall colors and see if they could find some late-hatched pollywogs. It would be fun to catch some and place them in a bucket of water, to watch them turn into frogs.

Ringo hadn't been ridden for a few weeks, so he was frisky in the cool morning air. Jim was having a little trouble with him. He pranced around and spooked at the slightest noise.

"Are you going to be able to handle Ringo?" Ben asked.

"I think so," Jim answered. "If he gets too feisty, we can go back to the road and run him some. That should take the friskiness out of him."

Ringo seemed to settle down as the boys rode across the field toward the creek. Jim's confidence increased and Ben became less nervous about the situation. Everything seemed to be going fine as they approached the creek bank. They rode down it, and just as they got to the bottom, Ringo began bucking. Jim wasn't prepared for that. "Whoa," he called, pulling on the reigns, trying to get his pony under control. He hung on for dear life, but was losing his grip. Ringo kicked just as Jim flipped backward off him. His left hoof caught Jim in the side of the head, sending him flying into the creek.

"Oh, no," cried Ben, as he scrambled off Jericho and ran to his friend. "Are you all right?"

Jim didn't answer.

Ben dragged his friend out of the creek and began trying to revive him. It wasn't working. He lay limp, obviously knocked out. Ben picked him up, staggered up the creek bank, and lugged him toward the house.

Mrs. Kellogg saw them coming and went to meet them. She took Jim, carried him into the house and laid him on the bed. Then she began trying to revive him. Nothing worked. She washed his face and talked to him. Then she tried smelling salts. Nothing. She couldn't get him revived.

"We'll have to take him to the doctor," she said. "Betty, go get your dad. Tell him to hitch the team to the wagon. We need to hurry."

As the Kelloggs prepared to take Jim to the doctor, Ben returned to the creek for their horses. They were standing quietly, with the reigns dangling on the ground, just as they were trained to do.

As the Kellogg family left for town, Ben headed home leading Jericho. He just couldn't get back on him, not after what had happened to his friend.

The next day, Mr. Kellogg came to the Parker's house. "How's Jim?" Ben asked.

"Not good," he answered. "He had an acute concussion. He didn't wake up until this morning. We don't know how bad it is yet."

Ben had a worried look. He turned and walked away with tears in his eyes. What if his friend never got over this accident?

Jim never completely recovered from the ordeal. The blow to his head caused severe brain damage. Never again would he play with his special buddy the way they once did. Ben was extremely hurt and traumatized by the outcome of his friend's accident.

"I will never again ride a horse," Ben declared.

And he never did!

GRANDPA

Grandpa at Work
Even in his old age, Ben's grandpa was a hard worker.
He often helped Doc with the chores around the
house, as well as on his truck farm.

"I got a letter from your grandpa Parker today," Doc announced, as the family finished eating supper.

"I thought Grandpa could not read or write," Sherod said.

"He can't. He got his neighbor, James Harrison, to write it for him."

"What did he have to say?" Daniel questioned.

"He hasn't been able to work for a couple of years and his bronchitis is getting worse. He was wondering if the climate here in Brock might help improve his illness. He and your grandma are thinking of moving here."

"Can I see the letter?" Ben asked.

"Sure, I'll get it for you."

When Doc returned from his bedroom, he handed the letter to Ben. "Think you can read it?"

"You bet. I'm eight and in the second grade. I can read it."

Ben took the letter and read each word carefully.

April 10, 1895

Dear Doc,

My name is James Harrison and I am a neighbor of your father, E. M. Parker. He asked me to write the following letter to you. From now on, the words I write will be his words.

To Benjamin Franklin (Doc) Parker

For the past two years, I have been unable to work due to old age and bronchitis, which I have had for 11 years. Also, my eyesight is failing me. I had a bad winter this past year. My bronchitis was made worse by the very wet winter. I know you and Alice moved to Brock in 1881 to get her in a dryer climate because of her bronchitis. Did it help? Do you think moving to Brock would help me?

I'm not looking for a handout. I would do whatever I could to help you, but it wouldn't be much. Do you know of a small place where your mother and I could live? We can't afford much rent. We have a little money saved up, and I have a note on the farming equipment and horses I sold two years ago. It brings in $35.00 a year plus interest at 10%.

I am looking forward to hearing from you soon.

Sincerely, your father,

E. M. X (His mark) Parker

"I'm going to answer his letter tomorrow. I want you boys to help build them a small house on the back of our property. We'll place the front door on the other road that runs by our place. Daniel, I'd like you and Sherod to go to Weatherford tomorrow and get a load of lumber.

Then, I'd like the two of you to start work on the house as soon as possible."

"But, I need to look for a job," Daniel replied. "I need to start saving for a place of my own. Effie and I are planning on getting married in a couple of years."

"I was planning on paying you 20 cents an hour. That's about all you could get anywhere else. You're 18, and it's about time you started thinking about a place of your own. This job could help you get started."

"Would I get paid, too?" Sherod asked.

"Of course. You're 16 and plenty old enough to make a good hand. Today is Monday, April 15. I'd like to have the house ready by the middle of July. That will give Mom and Dad enough time to wrap up any business they have there and get here."

"What can I do?" Ben asked.

"You and Ed can keep the construction site clean. You can work on it after school and Saturdays. When school is out next month, Ed can help with the construction, and you can continue keeping the area clean. I'll help when I can get away from the store."

"I can't wait for Grandpa and Grandma to get here," Ben stated. "I like them. It'll be great having them living so close to us."

The boys worked diligently on the house for the three months Doc had allotted them. By the second week in July, the finishing touches were added. It was a small, two-room abode, much the same as the sharecropper houses in the area around Brock. In one room, there was a wood-burning heater. A small living area was laid out along one wall. A bed, flanked by two nightstands, were placed near the opposite wall. The front door opened out onto a small yard, which bordered on the road at the back side of Doc's property.

The other room served as a kitchen and dining area. A wood-burning cook stove stood near the middle of one wall. Beside it was a cupboard with an area for preparing food. Along the opposite wall, toward the back of the room, stood a dining table and four chairs. A rear door opened onto a back yard, with enough room for a chicken coop or a rabbit hutch. It was a modest house with humble furnishings but sufficient for their needs at the time.

Doc and his wife, Alice, along with the eight children left at home, were anxiously awaiting the arrival of Doc's parents, Edward Marion and Martha Ann Parker.

About noon on Thursday, July 18, Ben heard a wagon pull into their yard. He went running into the house. "Grandpa and Grandma are here," he shouted.

The family filed out to greet them. "We're so glad to see you," Alice said. "It's been a long time."

"Too long," Edward replied. "Where's Doc?"

"At the store."

"What store?"

"He has a general mercantile store here in Brock. That business, along with this orchard and truck farm, keeps him pretty busy. Minnie, go get your poppa. Daniel can take care of things while he comes over to greet his parents."

"How big is Doc's orchard and truck farm?" Edward asked.

"He has 80 acres in all. The orchard is 20 acres and the truck farm is 10 acres," Alice answered."

"We didn't bring much with us," Edward said. "We sold most of our furniture to lighten the load."

"Don't worry," Ben responded. "Your house is finished, and it's furnished."

Ben was beaming. It had been four years since he had seen his grandparents. Since his grandpa didn't have to work, he planned to spend lots of time with him. Maybe the two of them could go fishing. He sidled up to Edward and took his hand. It was a hand that obviously had seen many years of labor. Rough calluses were prominent on the palm. The fingers were slightly gnarled from age and the effects of arthritis. *These hands show character*, Ben thought. *I wonder how many plows or hoe handles they've held.*

"Let's go in and get some dinner," Alice suggested. "It's almost ready, and we don't want it to get cold."

About the time they sat down, Doc arrived. Hugs and laughter were plentiful as he and his parents embraced for the first time in four years.

"How was your trip?" Doc asked.

"Great," his father, Edward, answered. "We didn't have any trouble. The weather was a little hot, but the covering over the wagon shaded us most of the time."

After dinner, Ben, Ed and Sherod helped their grandparents move into their new home.

"Wow, this is great," Edward said. "I've never slept on a new bed before."

"I've never cooked on a new stove," Martha said.

Doc was a devout Methodist and took his family to church almost every Sunday. After his parents moved to Brock, they also attended the Methodist church with Doc and his family. In a short time, Edward and Martha were considered an important part of the congregation. The pastor and parishioners liked them, and they were invited to all church functions.

After a few weeks, Edward began noticing his grandson, Ben, listening intently to the pastor's sermons. One Friday, while they were fishing, Edward asked, "Ben, have you accepted Jesus as your Lord and Savior?"

"Not yet, but I've been thinking about it."

"I think you need to go down to the altar when the preacher gives the call Sunday. If you're nervous, I'll go down with you."

"Thanks, Grandpa. I'll sure think about it."

On Sunday, Edward and Ben walked down to the altar, hand-in-hand. It was the beginning of a new life for Ben. He had never felt such peace and contentment before. He and his grandpa left the church that day, each wearing broad, beaming smiles.

It had been about two years since Edward and Martha moved to Brock. One afternoon, they heard a carriage pull into their front yard. Martha went to the window.

"It looks like Lilla," she said.

Edward peered out the window. "It is Lilla. I wonder why she's here."

Edward and Martha went to the door to greet their daughter. It was a pleasant surprise. They had no idea she was coming to visit them.

"Did you drive that carriage all the way from Leon County?" Edward asked.

"No, I caught the train to Weatherford. I rented this hack from a livery stable there."

"Come in," Martha said. "Sit down and rest."

"I've been sitting down for about 16 hours. I need to stand up for a while."

"Have you had dinner?"

"Yes, I ate at that road house outside Weatherford. The food wasn't that great, but it was filling. I'll be just fine until suppertime."

The three of them spent the rest of the afternoon talking about old times and reminiscing about events from their past. It was evident that Martha was extremely pleased with Lilla's visit. She seemed happier than she had been since they moved to Brock. Her laughter filled their modest house. She loved every minute of her visit with her daughter.

Lilla visited for a few days, and then announced, "I need to get back home. I'll be leaving in the morning, and I'm taking the two of you back with me."

"You're not taking me with you," Edward said.

"Oh, don't be such an old fuddy duddy," Lilla retorted. "Leon County is your home and has been for 23 years. You belong back there."

"This is my home now. There's nothing in Leon County that I am attached to."

"I live there. Don't you want to be near your daughter and grandchildren?"

"My bronchitis is too bad there. I wouldn't last two more years if I go back."

"I think I'd like to go back with Lilla," Martha said.

"And leave me?"

"If that's what it takes to get back home."

Edward's sleep was fitful that night. His world was falling apart. His wife of 50 years was leaving him. He thought of the golden anniversary they had celebrated in April, but his mind was made up. He just couldn't go back to the wet, humid climate in Eastern Texas. His bronchitis was better at Brock. Back there, it would gradually get worse. Maybe he could talk Martha out of going.

After breakfast the next morning, Lilla and Martha began loading Martha's belongings into the carriage. It was obvious that Edward would not be able to talk his wife out of leaving. He didn't even try.

Just before the loading was complete, Lilla stopped in front of the painting of her mother that hung on the living room wall. "I'm taking that picture back with me."

"No, you're not," Edward retorted. "I paid Abe Jones a week's wages for him to paint that picture of your mother when she was 27. It belongs to me, and you're not taking it."

"You old coot," Lilla shouted. "You don't have any need for that picture. You're almost blind now and it won't be long until you won't even be able to see it. I'm taking it!"

Edward turned and left through the back door. It wasn't his nature to stand and argue with anyone. As he walked to the back gate, he saw Ben a few feet away, picking June corn to sell at the store.

"Come here, Ben," he called. "I need you to do something for me."

Ben sat his bucket down and came to him. "What is it, Grandpa?"

"Your Aunt Lilla insists that she is going to take the picture of your grandma back to Centerville. I need you to go get Doc and let him straighten this thing out."

"It's done," Ben said, then headed to the store in a run.

When Doc arrived a few minutes later, Lilla had the picture in the carriage and was about to leave. "Put that picture back on the wall," Doc ordered.

"I will not!" Lilla answered. "This old man doesn't need that picture, and I'm taking it with me."

"You'll put it back, or I'll send for Sheriff Baxter and have you arrested."

"I'm leaving," Lilla shouted.

"Go ahead and leave. Sheriff Baxter will find you. Parker County is a big county, and the sheriff has deputies in every city. All he has to do is wire ahead, and you will be thrown in jail for theft."

Lilla had a scowl on her face as she tossed the painting on the ground. "You can go to the devil, Benjamin Franklin Parker. I'll never speak to you again."

"If that's what you want, it's all right with me. If that's what it takes to keep you from riding rough-shod over Dad, then so be it."

Lilla popped the horse's rump with the reigns and left in a cloud of dust.

GRANDPA'S PENSION

Confederate Soldier's Pension Approval for Edward Marion Parker.
Ben's grandpa received a pension under that law, as described in this
chapter.
Notice that approved is spelled "approoved".

On Sunday, July 30, 1899, Edward came home from church with Doc and his family. As they were having their Sunday dinner, Ben asked, "Grandpa, did you see the article in the Weatherford Democrat last Friday about the Texas Confederate Soldiers and Sailors Pension Law?"

"No, I can hardly read anymore. I don't take the Democrat," Edward answered.

"The law was passed May 12 of this year," Ben said. "You were in the Civil War, weren't you?"

"Yes, I was. I served about two years."

"Then you should be eligible for the pension. I think you should apply."

Edward thought for a minute. "I don't know. Do you think I might qualify?"

"It won't hurt to try," Ben replied. "Wasn't R. J. McKenzie in the Civil War with you?"

"Yes, he was maybe 15 years younger than me, about 23 at the time. He was going to school to be a lawyer when they inducted him."

"He's an attorney in Weatherford now, Grandpa. Maybe you should go see him. He should be able to tell you if you're entitled to the pension."

"I have something important to do tomorrow," Doc stated. "I'll be glad to take you to Weatherford Tuesday to see R. J. If you're eligible for the pension, we can get things going."

"Alright," Edward answered. "I could use a little more income."

On Tuesday of that week, Doc and Edward went to Weatherford in Doc's buggy. Their first stop was at the office of R. J. McKenzie, Attorney at Law. He recognized Edward at once.

"Hello, E. M.," he said. "It's been a long time. How have you been?"

"Very good, under the circumstances," Edward answered. "How about you?"

"Can't complain. What brings you to Weatherford?"

"I heard about the Confederate Pension Law, and want to check and see if I qualify."

"I need to ask you a few questions," R. J. responded. "Let me get the pension form number one. May as well be filling it out while you answer the questions."

He reached behind him and retrieved the form from his shelf.

"I know you were in the Civil War. I was with you in the 6th Alabama Cavalry Regiment, Company A. How long have you lived in Texas?"

"Since December, 1869, Edward replied. "That's almost 30 years."

"You live in Brock now. How long have you lived there?"

"Four years."

"How's your health, E. M.?"

"Not good," Edward answered. "I've had bronchitis for 15 years, and infirmity of age, and I'm almost blind, can see but little."

R. J. read the next question. "How much income do you have?"

"I get $35.00 a year plus interest on a $350.00 note."

"Do you own any property in the form of real estate?"

"No, Edward answered. "I'm living in Doc's house. I own none myself."

"From what I can tell, you qualify," R. J. said. "Let's finish filling out this form, then you can take it over to Judge Roach and get it filed."

The attorney finished the form, asking Edward questions at the appropriate places. When it was completed, he had Edward sign his X, and handed it to him.

Doc and Edward left the law office and drove to the Weatherford County Courthouse. Tying the horse to the hitching post, they entered the building. Walking down the long corridor, they found an office with the sign J. N. Roach, County Judge over the door. Entering, they saw Judge Roach sitting on the far side of a large conference table.

"Good afternoon, Doc," the judge said. "What brings you to Weatherford?"

"I've brought my dad to apply for a Confederate soldier's pension. This is my dad, Edward Parker. Dad, this is Judge Roach."

"Glad to meet you, Mr. Parker. Do you have form number one?"

"Yes," Edward answered. "I just came from my attorney's office. He filled it out for me."

The judge took the form and looked it over. "Mmm, everything seems to be in order. Let's get things started. You'll need at least two witnesses. Doc, do you know for sure that E. M. was in the Civil War?"

"Yes, I was 13 when he enlisted."

"Then you can sign as one witness. If you can get three or four other witnesses, his chances of getting the pension will be improved."

Finishing their business in Weatherford, Doc and Edward drove back to Brock. They arrived just before suppertime.

"How did it go?" Ben asked.

"Quite well, I thought," Edward answered. "I need to get three or four witnesses to testify that I was in the war."

"Do you know where some of your Civil War buddies are?" Ben questioned.

"Yes, several of them live in Texas, and one lives in Alabama. There's also my oldest son, T. J. He lives in West Texas."

"I can help you. I'm 12 and have good handwriting. I can write the letters for you."

"Thank you, Ben. That's nice of you. I can use all the help I can get."

Over the next three months, letters were sent out and depositions gathered. The last one was taken on November 9, 1899. Then came the long process of cross examination and court hearings. Finally, on March 14, 1900 the pension was granted.

Ben was extremely glad he had been a small part in helping his grandpa get his pension. When the first check came, he was as excited as his grandpa. "How much did you get?" Ben questioned.

"I got $23.30," Edward answered.

"Let's see. With your note payment, that makes about $73.30 for the year."

"Exactly. How did you figure that out so quick?"

"I'm very good with figures in my head. That's not very much, is it? The average wage for a year is about $300.00."

"No, but I'm grateful to get that much. I can make it do for my needs."

A few weeks later, Ben and his grandpa were fishing on the banks of the Brazos River. As they sat, drowning worms and talking, Ben remarked, "Grandpa, I've been going over the depositions. James Roach states in his that you were captured during the Civil War and taken to Ship Island. I didn't know that. You never talk about it."

"It's too painful," Edward answered. "I don't want to remember that part of my life."

"It would be nice to hear about it. I wouldn't tell anyone."

Ben put another worm on his hook. Edward checked his hook, then said, "Alright, I'll tell you a little about it. I was captured in December, 1864, and sent to Ship Island, Mississippi. The living conditions there were not good. We had to live on the parade ground in worn out tents and sleep on the ground using old, ragged blankets. We didn't get any new clothes for three months, and when they arrived, they too were old and almost worn out. Our rations were in short supply, and often were not edible. All in all, it was a bad situation. That's why I don't talk about it. I just want to forget, but I can't. I just keep it bottled up inside me."

"Thank you for telling me," Ben said. "No one will ever hear about that experience from me."

They fished in silence for a few minutes.

"Let's talk about something more pleasant," Ben said. "Tell me about the time Poppa slept with the wild hogs."

"You've heard that story a dozen times," Edward answered with a hearty laugh.

"I know, but I never get tired of hearing it."

"Okay. If you get bored with it, just stop me."

When Doc and Alice got married in Alabama, on Independence Day in 1872, they left right away for Texas. Doc had a black-and-tan hound named Rex. He was a good coon dog, and Doc liked to hunt coon, so he took the dog with him. When he got to Texas, you hardly saw him at night during coon season.

One night, a cold Texas norther blew in not long after he and Rex left for their hunt. About the time the norther hit, Rex barked treed. Doc went to him, and he had a coon treed on the banks of the Navasota River. When he walked up to the tree, the coon jumped in the river, as coons will do. Rex jumped in after him. That was the wrong thing to do. A coon will drown a dog in the water.

The coon got on Rex's head and was about to drown him. Doc wasn't about to let that happen. He picked up a stick, grabbed a willow branch and leaned out over the river to knock the coon off Rex's head. The branch he caught hold of was dead. It broke and dumped Doc in the water.

Doc and Rex, both soaking wet, left the coon and started to the house in a fast walk. That cold norther had them almost frozen. They needed to get to a warm place fast.

On the way to the house, they passed a cliff about 40 feet high. On the south side of the cliff, a pack of wild hogs was bedded down in a thick pile of blackjack and post oak leaves. It hadn't rained yet, so the leaves were dry. The hogs got up and chased Rex. He ran for the house as fast as he could go.

Thinking the hogs had left for good, Doc laid down in those warm leaves where the hogs had been and pulled them over him. He was cold and needed to get warm.

Just about the time he got comfortable, the hogs returned and bedded down all around him. He was afraid to move, so he just lay still all night.

About daybreak, the hogs got up and started feeding. As soon as they left, Doc got up and went home.

Ben chuckled. "That's really is a funny story. I can hear Momma teasing Poppa right now about sleeping with the hogs."

"She also says about the only grease she had to cook with for the first three years of their marriage was coon grease."

Edward and Ben left for home, glad for another day spent together. They had a few fish, enough for one good meal. That didn't matter. Being together did.

One day the next spring, Ben and Doc were working in the store. Ben was quiet, obviously in deep contemplation. "A penny for your thoughts," Doc said.

"I was thinking about Grandma going back to East Texas without Grandpa. Poppa, why did Grandma do that to Grandpa?"

"Don't be too hard on your grandma," Doc answered. "She didn't like Brock. She was homesick from the minute she got here. When Lilla said she was taking them back, she jumped at the chance. I blame Lilla more than Mother. When she saw Dad wasn't going with her, she should have backed off, and not split them up that way. But Lilla has always been like that. She thinks of no one but herself."

"Even so, I'm sorry Grandma went back."

"Me, too. I miss her, but she has a mind of her own."

On Friday, May 24, 1901, Ben graduated from grammar school. He was the first of Doc's children to do so. His older brothers and sisters had dropped out of school before graduation.

The next night, as the family was having supper, Ben's grandpa Edward gave him an admiring look. "I'm proud of you for graduating from grammar school. None of my kids and few of my grandkids have graduated. Some of them didn't go to school at all."

"What do you plan to do with your life?" Doc questioned.

"I'm going to be a farmer," Ben replied.

"Let me make a suggestion. Why don't you be a schoolteacher? You would have to go to college for one semester and take a class called Teaching Methods. I'd pay for it."

"I don't want to be a teacher. I want to be a farmer."

"Teaching would be much easier," Alice said. "And you would have summers off. You could do farming on the side."

"I'm not a teacher. I'm a farmer."

"Okay," Doc answered. "What you do with your life is your business, not mine. But I do have one more suggestion. Old man Johnston's 50 acres across the road is fallow this year. He's too old to farm it. You could probably rent it for $50.00 a year, payable when the crops are harvested. That would give you a start."

"Thanks for the information," Ben said. "I'll contact him and try to make a deal."

"In the meantime, you can work for me in the store and the truck farm. I can use you only part time, but at least you would have some money coming in."

"Thanks, I'll do that."

Edward drew his pension for four years. His last payment was in June of 1903. It was $37.00. That year was also the last payment he received on the $350.00 note. It was $38.50. The next winter, on January 23, 1904, Edward Marion Parker passed away. Ben was sad, but thankful he had almost 10 years of close fellowship with a grandpa he loved.

A few months later, Ben and Doc were working in the store. "How would you like to live in Dad's house?" Doc asked.

"That would be fine with me," Ben answered.

"It could be your bachelor house. It will go downhill if someone isn't using it. That would give both of your younger brothers a room of their own. At 12, Bob is not too keen on sharing a room with his younger brother. You could take all your meals with us, if you like. Or, you could cook in your new house."

"Okay, I'll move my things tomorrow."

The next day, Ben gathered his personal belongings and moved into his bachelor house. When suppertime came, he went back to eat with his family.

"Mama, the picture of Grandma that used to be on the living room wall is gone. Did you burn it with the rest of the trash from their house?" Ben asked.

"Let's just say your poppa and I got rid of it. I don't think Lilla will ever come back for it, but if she does, she can't take what's not here."

"I liked that picture."

"I did, too. Getting rid of it was our way of burning the bridges between us and our kin in East Texas. I don't care if we never see them again."

The next year, on September 4, 1905, Ben's grandma, Martha Ann Parker, passed away. Lilla persuaded the rest of the family in East Texas to keep the news from Doc and his family. Two months later, Doc got a letter from a sister in Oklahoma. She told him about the death of his mother.

"How is it possible for Grandpa to be so nice, and one of his daughters be so cruel?" Ben asked.

COURTSHIP

Ben and Tildie on their wedding day, Sunday, June 4, 1905

Ben at age 16, in the year 1902   Tildie at age 16, in the year 1904

"Poppa, I met the prettiest gal last night at the church social," Ben said.

"Oh," Doc answered. "What's her name?"

"Matildie Lee Bratcher, but her friends call her Tildie. She goes to the Baptist church, but she came to the social with her friend, June Thompson."

"That would be Sandy Bratcher's girl. She's a looker all right, and she comes from a fine family. They don't make them any better than Sandy."

"I really like her. Not only is she pretty, but she has a great personality. She could be the one for me. I just hope she feels the same way."

"You could do much worse."

On that Monday morning, February 20, 1905, Doc and Ben were opening the store and getting ready for business. Doc looked at his son. He had never seen him so starry-eyed before. *Could he be falling in love? In the spring, a young man's heart turns to thoughts of love. But it isn't spring yet.*

All that day, Ben seemed distracted. Doc had to tell him to do things he normally would do on his own. Near the end of the day, Doc said, "Are you thinking about your new-found lady friend?"

"Yes, I can't get her off my mind. What should I do?"

"Court her. If she's the one for you, everything will be okay."

Ben was silent for a minute. "I think I'll go to her house after work today."

"Will you be home for supper?" Doc asked.

"I don't know," Ben responded. "It depends on how things work out."

"Just don't be out too late. Tomorrow is another work day."

Ben began spending a lot of time with Tildie. If she really was the one, he didn't want her to slip through his fingers. Most of their time together was spent at her folks' house, but they occasionally went on dates to parties and other places. He was at the Bratcher home so much that her mother, Betty, began joking, "Ben is around here so much, I can't even throw out the dishwater without hitting him in the face with it."

Ben picked Tildie up in the family buggy every Sunday morning and took her to church. The first time they attended services together, Ben asked, "Which church do you want to go to?"

"Yours. When the man and woman are both Christians, I think the woman should go to the man's church."

On Saturday, March 18, almost a month after they met, Ben drove the buggy to her house. "How would you like to go on a picnic today?" he asked.

"I'd love it. I can pack us a lunch. Where would we go?"

"How about the Brazos River? I know a great spot for a picnic. Grandpa and I used to go fishing there. It's beautiful."

"Sounds great to me. I'll have the lunch ready in a few minutes."

On the drive to the river, Tildie scooted close to Ben and took his hand. "I love being with you. You're such a gentleman and I always have a good time."

"I love being with you, too," Ben answered. "You're the prettiest thing I ever saw and I also have fun when we're together."

The picnic at the river was great. The lovers gazed into each other's eyes all the time they were eating. Later, they walked along the river hand-in-hand, then sat on a rock, dangling their feet in the water. Ben looked into Tildie's dark brown eyes. "Would you consider being my wife?" he asked.

"Yes I would," she replied. "But you'll need to ask Papa for my hand in marriage."

Ben smiled, obviously pleased. "I'll do that as soon as we get you home."

"What day should we get married?" Tildie asked.

"How about Sunday, June 4?"

"That would be great. I'll be 17 by then."

Ben was ecstatic. A beautiful, vibrant, loving young lady had just agreed to marry him. He could hardly contain his enthusiasm.

When Ben returned home, he was beaming. "Why are you looking so happy?" Alice asked.

"Tildie just agreed to be my wife."

"That's great. I like her and she's from a good family."

The next day, after the church service, Reverend Jerry Brown came to Ben. "I've been noticing you," he said. "You are very knowledgeable about the Bible. I'd like you to teach the boy's Sunday school class. Their teacher moved away, and we need someone to take his place."

"I'd be glad to," Ben answered.

"I'll tell the superintendent we have someone. Could you start next Sunday?"

"Yes, I can. Do you have Sunday school books, or will I be teaching from the Bible?"

"We have Sunday school literature," Reverend Brown answered. "Come with me to the office and I'll get a teacher's copy for you."

The next day, while working in Doc's store, Ben said, "Poppa, I've been thinking about going to work at the brickyard. Tildie and I are getting married, and I could use the extra money. I can make 30 cents an hour there. That's 10 cents more than I make here. Uncle Edward is foreman there and he says he can use me full time for two or three months. I'd be working six days a week, 10 hours a day."

"That's okay by me," Doc answered. "You can use the extra money to get you and Tildie started. When you get through working there, you always have a job here."

Ben was very busy for a few months. Even so, he took time to see Tildie several nights a week. He also set aside a few hours each week to study the Sunday school lesson he was to teach the boys in his class. Tildie understood. She was happy her man was involved in church work. She also knew that his long hours at the brick yard would help them set up housekeeping. She had really fallen in love with him, and was counting the days until their wedding.

On Monday, May 8, Sandy Bratcher had to go to the brick yard. Tildie went with him. While Sandy was buying some bricks for a project he was doing, Tildie spotted Ben and waved to him. Ben left his work and came over to her. They began playing around, laughing and having a good time. Tildie pulled a bulrush and whacked Ben on the rump. He pulled one and the two of them began a heated game of rap jack. Ben's Uncle Edward saw them and yelled, "Hey, Ben, get over here. We're not paying you to play around."

Ben looked dejected. "I have to get back to work."

"That's okay," Tildie responded. "I think Papa is about ready to go."

She handed him a letter and went back to the wagon she and her Papa had come in. They waved goodbye and left for home.

The next evening, Tildie's cousin delivered a letter to her. When she opened it, she could tell it was from Ben. She recognized his handwriting. She lay back on the bed and read it.

Brock Texas
May 9. 05

Miss Tildie Bratcher

My kind darling I will answer your loving letter it was the best and lovingist letter that ever I read, it reached deep down in my heart for it was from my dearest darling, The truest and lovingist darling living and the prettiest one living,

Tildie if I could tell how well I love you this tablet would not hold all the words, and it would take me along time to write this loving letter, say darling I dident do what I said I would about that fan I dident give it to you, of course I had as soon for you to have the fan as me for I know it will be takend care of better than if I would keep it,

Darling you asked me if that whipping hurt, of course it dident; I hope I did not hurt you when I were whipping you, for they were love liks, I wouldent of hit you to hurt for this house full of money for I love you to well to hurt your feeling's in any way.

Say darling how did you enjoy yourself yesterday I sure seen a fine time, darling I couldent hardly part from you to go to work, if Edd will think about when he was young he wont care for me resting when you are here, for if he loved Susie as well as I love you he couldent care, say darling I will be glad when the time comes when you and I wont hafe to part and go home, and this will be your home and that will be my home,

Say darling you asked me if that wasent my home Sunday evening it isent know but I dont care how soon it will be when I can call that my home, sweetheart Minnie say's you and I will hafe to have that over so she can come, and see us after we get married, Even if your home is not my home now, It would of suited me alright if it had of been so,

Say dear it is raining know I hope it wont be raining when the time comes for us to go to the concert, say darling I seen Mr Dent this morning and he was surprised he thought I was married and Robert Harrison asked me if I were married and Lee Head asked me if I loved you and I told him yes.

Ben continued working at the brickyard and spending most of his free time with Tildie. On Sunday, May 28, he went home with her after church and helped celebrate her seventeenth birthday. It was just one week from their wedding date. He was extremely happy, as was Tildie. They were now counting the hours until the big moment.

On Sunday, June 4, 1905, Ben and Tildie said their wedding vows. It was a simple ceremony in the home of her parents. Reverend Brown officiated. Afterward, the young couple rode off in the family buggy to begin their new life together.

FAMILY MATTERS

Peanut Harvest, Brock, Texas 1916
The man on the right holding the pitchfork is Ben's father-in-law, the owner.
Ben is at the far right, driving a team of horses.
During the first part of the twentieth century,
everyone pitched in to harvest the crops.

Ben and Tildie quickly settled into married life. Doc allowed them to live in the house he built for his dad. Ben continued farming the 50 acres he had rented from Mr. Johnston for the past four years. He also worked part-time for Doc, both in the store and the truck farm. He was very faithful to teach the boys' Sunday school class at the Methodist church. He was deliriously happy and was a good husband to Tildie.

Farming was a difficult trade. It was sometimes dusty and dirty work, but rewarding. Ben loved to see plants grow; plants he had sown as seeds. With joy, he donned his bib-overalls or his loose-fitting trousers held up by suspenders and took to the fields. Loose clothing allowed the breeze to circulate better in the hot Texas sun. He loved the excitement of watching his creations mature into usable food for his family or his livestock. He thrilled at his harvest, gathering in his bounty, as the Bible says, "… some an hundredfold, some sixtyfold, some thirtyfold."

When the fieldwork was done, Ben's day was still far from over. Other chores awaited. The livestock had to be fed. The cows required milking. Things needed to be repaired. Tildie helped with the chores, and, in return, Ben helped with the dishwashing each night. He sometimes even cooked. They worked together as a team. Neither thought of the other's job as men's work; or women's work. They worked together. Tildie sometimes even helped in the fields. She could operate a planter for Ben during planting season, thus saving him time.

A little less than two years after their marriage, on March 22, 1907, their firstborn arrived, a boy. They named him Francis William, and began the unending task of caring for him. Tildie turned out to be a good mother, as well as a loving wife. When he was not working on the farm, Ben helped Tildie with Francis. He changed diapers, fed him, rocked him to sleep and did any other chore that needed to be done. His mother had taught him well in that area.

About three months after Francis was born, Reverend Brown stopped Ben after church. "I have something I need to discuss with you. I've been watching you in the boys' class. You have a good speaking voice, as well as a thorough knowledge of the Bible. I'd like you to consider taking the position of layman in our church."

"What would that position require?"

"It's a voluntary job. You would help me with visitation one day a month, and preach for me when I need to be gone on church business. You wouldn't be paid a salary as such, but we would take an offering for you about twice a year."

Ben hesitated for a moment. "I hadn't thought about that. I would have to pray about it."

"Please give it some serious thought. Would one week be enough time for you to make up your mind?"

"Yes, I can give you an answer next Sunday."

After their Sunday dinner, Tildie observed Ben sitting in the rocking chair. He seemed preoccupied, as if his mind was 1,000 miles away.

"What are you thinking about?" she asked.

"Pastor Brown offered me the position of Layman in the church."

"What would that require?"

"I would help him with visitation and preach when he is gone."

Tildie stopped washing dishes. Looking at Ben, she asked, "Are you going to take it?"

"I don't know yet. I have to pray about it and give it a lot of thought."

"When do you have to give him an answer?"

"Next Sunday."

Tildie returned to her kitchen work. "My thoughts right now are you should take it."

"If God doesn't close the door by Sunday, I'll probably take the job."

The next Sunday, Ben saw Reverend Brown standing on the church porch, shaking hands with everyone who entered. "I've prayed about your offer. If it is still open, I would like to take the job."

"Excellent. Could you go with me on a couple of visits next Saturday?"

"I don't have anything planned. I'd be glad to accompany you."

Ben began the routine of helping Pastor Brown. About two months later, Tildie's parents came into Brock on Saturday to buy supplies. While there, they went to see Tildie. Ben was with his pastor, visiting some sick people.

"Ben is preaching in the Methodist Church tomorrow," Tildie said.

"I didn't know he was a preacher," Sandy answered.

"He just started. He is now a layman in the church."

"When does church start?" he asked.

"After Sunday school is over. About 10:30."

Sandy looked at his wife. "Betty, is it all right for us to go to the Methodist Church tomorrow?"

"Sure, it is. I'd like to hear Ben preach."

That Sunday, Ben surprised the congregation by having Tildie play the organ for the service. She hadn't had any music lessons: just an ear for the right notes and chords for the songs she knew. From that moment on, whenever the organist was absent, Tildie played for the church services.

After church on Sunday, Betty said, "Ben, I really enjoyed your sermon. I had no idea you were a preacher."

Ben smiled. "You mean a beginning preacher, don't you?"

"And a good one," Betty said proudly.

"How about coming home with us for dinner?" Ben asked.

"I'd love to. I'll ask Sandy."

After dinner, Sandy and Ben were talking. "Is this a paying position?" Sandy asked.

"No, it's voluntary, but the church will give me an offering about twice a year."

"No mind. It's good to see you serving the church in any position. I'm proud of you."

Ben and Tildie continued living in Doc's small, two-room house for the next nine years. With their overwhelming happiness, they would be satisfied anywhere. Their second child, a girl, was born there on April 23, 1911. They named her Alice Gertrude, and called her by her middle name.

In the spring of 1912, Pink White came into Doc's store. "I heard you are wanting to sell this store," he said.

"Yes, I am," Doc answered. "Are you in the market for a store?"

"I sure am. I got some money through an inheritance, and I'm looking for something for an investment. How much do you want for it?"

"Make me an offer," Doc responded.

After a little haggling, they came to an agreement and Doc sold his store. At 62 years of age, he was ready to slow down. Besides, he had another venture he would like to try. He was harvesting good crops from his orchard and truck farm. He was going into the canning business.

The next day, Doc came to visit Ben and Tildie. "I sold my store," he said.

"Oh," Ben responded. "Did you get a good price for it?"

"I got what I consider a fair deal."

"Are you going to retire?"

"No, I'm going into the canning business. I'd like you to help me part time, just during the canning season."

Ben considered the offer. "Yes, I'll help you. I'll have to learn how. Will you buy fruits and vegetables for canning, or will you use what you grow here?"

"I'll use what I grow here. There's no need to put out any more money."

The next day, Doc took his horses and wagon into Weatherford to buy the canning supplies he needed. He purchased a steam vat that would hold four racks with 24 cans on each rack. Then he bought a 40-gallon cast iron kettle, cans with lids and sweat solder. Returning home, he set up his canning shop. Since he didn't have a shed large enough to be used as a cannery, he set it up in the shade of a large oak tree in his back yard. He now had a shade-tree food-processing shop.

For canning Doc's fruits and vegetables, they first used the cast iron kettle to cook the food. Then, they placed the processed food in the cans and sweat-soldered the lid on each one. Each lid had a small hole in the middle. After attaching the caps, they placed the containers on the racks in the steam vat. When steam began emerging from the holes, they sat a rack of cans on a table and put a drop of solder in the hole of each cover.

Doc had a younger brother who owned and operated the Parker Hotel in Mineral Wells, Texas. It was about 20 miles from Brock. When Dock and Ben had a load of canned goods, Doc took the back two seats out of his surrey and loaded it with the canned items. Early the next morning, he hitched his team to his buggy and headed for Mineral Wells. He had two rather large Tennessee Trotters, and they would make the trip in about an hour. He would sell canned goods the rest of that day, rent a room in his brother's hotel for the night, and sell the next day, until time for him to return home. His brother took what was left, used what he could in his hotel, and tried to peddle the rest. On the next trip, Doc's brother paid him for what he used and gave him the money for what he sold.

Ben worked with Doc on a part-time basis in that business for the next five years. At that time, the Texas legislature passed a law forbidding shade-tree canning operations. That put Doc out of business.

According to The Handbook of Texas Online, commercial production of peanuts began about 1906 in Texas. That year, about five carloads of peanuts were sold to a peanut oil, peanut butter and peanut confectionery at Paris in Lamar County. It was the first such factory in the state. In 1907, about 30 carloads were produced. The next year saw production increased to 150 carloads. In 1909, Texas farmers harvested 48,000 acres of peanuts with a yield of 26,400,000 pounds.

During the period from 1910 to 1914, the area where Ben's in-laws lived had an average yield of about 75 bushels of peanuts per acre. In addition, each acre produced about one and one-half tons of peanut hay. Peanuts brought 75 cents per bushel, and peanut hay about $12.00 a ton. Seed for planting averaged near $1.00 an acre. Each acre brought in a little over $70.00, not bad for farm income in those days.

By 1914, the net return per acre for a peanut crop exceeded that of cotton. When word got out about these yields, many farmers switched from growing cotton to the production of peanuts.

Starting in 1915, and for the next several years, Ben's father-in-law, Sandy Bratcher, planted peanuts. Sandy and Betty had a farm on the Brazos River, five miles south-west of Brock, which they bought when they first moved into that area. They didn't have as much sandy soil as the Lazy Bend of the Brazos, south of Weatherford, but they had enough to grow peanuts.

Ben always helped his father-in-law harvest his peanut crop. That's the way he was; always ready to help anyone. Since Sandy had a large farm to operate, he couldn't reciprocate, so he paid Ben for his work. It wouldn't have mattered. Ben would have helped him anyway, but Sandy paid him in order to help him support Tildie and the kids.

⚜

Ben and Tildie were happy in the little house on Doc's property. At that place, on January 8, 1913, their second son was born. They named him Roden Franklin. Then on November 22, 1914, another son, A T, was born.

As well as they liked it there, the house, more like a cottage, was becoming too small for their family. In the fall of 1916, Ben and Doc were canning peaches in the shade of the oak tree. Doc could tell his son was in deep thought. "What are you thinking about?" he asked.

"I've been thinking about moving. The house is too small for our family now, and Tildie is in a family way again. With a new baby, it will be very crowded."

"Where would you move to?"

"I've found a 60-acre farm at Authon. It has a four-room house and I can rent it for $60.00 a year. It's only about five miles from here. We would do our shopping in Garner or Peaster, but we would drive back here every Sunday for church. Authon doesn't have a church."

"You are an adult, and I can't tell you what to do. Just be sure you stay in church, and don't hesitate to contact me if you need anything."

In a few weeks, Ben and Tildie packed their belongings in a wagon and moved to their new home. As he promised, Ben continued attending the Brock Methodist Church as a layman. He seldom missed a service. Doc and Alice were always extremely happy to see them, and they often took Sunday dinner with Ben's parents.

While at Authon, their fifth child was born, on May 1, 1917. They named him Benjamin Artist and called him by his middle name.

As soon as the crops were harvested the next fall, they moved back to Brock. A long distance relationship with their family and church was too much for them. Ben found a farm about three-fourths of a mile from Brock. It had a four-room house, along with 70 acres of farming land. He could rent it for $70.00 a year, or 25% of the cash crops, whichever was greater. The family was much happier there, as were Doc and Alice.

They continued living in that house for the next 12 years. Four more children were born there. Male and female fraternal (dizygotic) twins, Earnest and Earnesteen, were born on November 16, 1919. Matilda Evelyn came on September 11, 1922. They called her Evelyn. Gladys Lavada was born on June 26, 1926. They called her Lavada. Also, while at that house, their oldest daughter, Alice Gertrude married Orville Robert Woodruff on December 23, 1923. She was only 12 years and five months old, but she was in love. She insisted she would elope if Ben and Tildie didn't give their permission. They relented.

There were some trying times at the house near Brock. On May 6, 1918, Tildie's mother, Emily Elizabeth (Betty) Bratcher, died. Ben comforted Tildie as only a loving husband can. "We know where she is," Ben said. "She was a good Christian lady, and there's no doubt she's in heaven."

"I know, but it still hurts."

"It will always hurt, and you will never forget her. Even if you live to be 100, you will still remember. Many years from now, you will be doing something and you'll suddenly stop and say, 'I'd like to see Mother again.'"

"Thank you, Ben. I feel better after talking about it."

In late spring of 1919, Ben and Francis were plowing one of the fields with Ben's team of mules. They were about to unhitch the mules for dinner. Francis walked up behind one of them and bent down to remove the chain from the single tree.

"Careful," Ben said. "Mules are unpredictable."

As soon as the chain rattled, the mule kicked. Francis reeled backward, clutching his head. Blood spurted from a puncture wound near the temple.

"Oh, no. Not again," Ben said.

Rushing to Francis's side, he quickly assessed the situation. His son was writhing in pain, going in and out of consciousness. Scooping him up into his arms, Ben hurriedly carried him to the house.

"Francis has been hurt," he said.

"How bad is it?" Tildie asked.

"Pretty bad. We need to get him to a doctor. I'll go get the mules and hitch them to the wagon while you get ready."

"Gertrude, will you feed the rest of the family?" Tildie asked. "Dinner's almost ready. We'll be back as soon as possible."

About two hours later, Ben and Tildie returned with Francis. His head was bandaged, but he was alert and smiling. Everyone rushed out to greet him.

"How's your head?" Roden asked.

"It hurts some, but it's okay."

"Are you going to be all right?"

"We have to watch him for a couple of days," Ben said. "If the pain gets worse, or if he gets a fever, we have to contact Doctor Larrin."

"Papa, I'm sorry I caused you so much trouble," Francis said. "I forgot that you told me to walk up to the mule from the side and pat his hip to let him know you're there. I'll never make that mistake again."

Francis recovered from his ordeal with the mule. The only lasting effects were headaches when he was stressed or worried about something.

That fall, Ben came in from harvesting corn. "Is dinner ready?" he asked.

"In a few minutes," Tildie said.

"Francis, will you and Roden go to the barn and shuck some corn for the horses. Feed them in the wagon so they won't waste the corn."

"Sure," Francis answered.

Of course, A T had to tag along. He was only four, but he thought he was as big as his brothers. Mostly, they liked to have him with them, but sometimes it became annoying.

When the boys had not returned within the time Ben thought they should, he went to the barn to find them. What he saw was both funny and exasperating at the same time. The three of them were sitting in the wagon, shelling corn on each other's heads. The horses were standing around the wagon, patiently waiting for them to stop so they could eat.

It was that incident which prompted Ben to come up with one of his short sayings. "One boy is a good boy. Two boys is a half boy. Three boys is no boy at all."

A couple of years after the accident with the mule, Francis acquired a saddle horse, which he named Duke. Francis rode him almost everywhere he went. It wasn't long until he discovered that Duke was a natural cutting horse. He had an uncanny ability to read the movements of a cow. Francis was suddenly in demand when the ranchers around Brock needed to doctor their cattle, brand them or cut out certain ones for market.

During the summer of 1923, Francis and some of his cousins met at the ranch of his Uncle Tom. He rode to Tom's house in a buggy with one of his cousins, so Duke was not with him. While there, Tom said, "Francis, if you can get Duke here, I would like for you to cut out a few head of cattle for me to take to market."

One of the cousins answered, "I have to take my little sis back home. I could ride by your house and tell Uncle Ben that you need Duke."

"That would be great," Francis answered. "Just ask Papa if he can saddle Duke and bring him over here."

About an hour later, Ben arrived, leading Duke.

"Papa, you just walked two and a half miles leading the best saddle horse in this county. Why didn't you ride him?"

"I'd rather walk."

Ben turned away. A flood of memories came over him; memories of his childhood friend, Jim Kellogg. It wasn't that he was trying to forget. He remembered Jim every time he saddled a horse. He just couldn't talk about it. The memories were extremely painful.

The summer of 1924, Francis left home and moved to Ada, Oklahoma. He rented a room from the Norton family and worked at the cement plant west of Ada. While there, he fell in love with their daughter, Dora Veda, and they were married on October 3, 1925. Ben and Tildie didn't get to attend the wedding. It was too far, and they were too busy harvesting their crops.

After the wedding, they moved to a small farm about two miles south of Bradley, Oklahoma. As soon as they were settled, Francis wrote a letter to his parents to let them know how they were and to give them their new address.

OKLAHOMA BOUND

Crossing the Red River in a covered wagon on a low-
water bridge, following the Chisholm Trail

Near the middle of June, 1928, Ben came in from the fields. "Tildie, I'd like to go to Oklahoma and visit Francis and his wife," he said. "They have a son, our first grandson, and we haven't even seen him yet."

"How far is it?"

"About 175 miles."

"How would we get there?" Tildie asked.

"In a wagon."

"Wouldn't that take a long time?"

Ben had a plan. He said, "With one team of horses, it would take about nine days. If we take two teams and work each team a half-day at a time, we could make it in six days."

"I'd like to see them, too, but what about our crops?"

"They're laid by. They won't need any attention for at least five or six weeks. We could drive there, stay about two weeks and let the horses rest, then drive back. We'd be back in about a month."

Tildie had a worried look. "A trip like that is a little scary."

"Yes, but we'll be alright. I've looked at a map and have it planned out. We can go northeast to Decatur and pick up the Chisholm Trail there. We'll follow it straight north to Marlow, Oklahoma, then turn east. There are several roads that lead to Lindsay from there. Francis lives about nine miles west of Lindsay."

Ben was in thought for a few seconds. "I'll need about a day to get everything ready. We can leave day after tomorrow."

The next day, Ben prepared the wagon for the trip. He put the seat in the front, then the frame and cover over the wagon. Next, he built a small cooler box to keep their food from spoiling in the heat. He placed a wooden box in the wagon for Tildie to pack the non-perishable food in, and another to hold the tarpaulin and the bedding. He placed several small wooden boxes along each side, for the children to sit on. Then he put in a few sticks of wood, in case they had to camp in a place with no deadwood. Last, he loaded two bales of hay and a sack of oats in the back to feed the horses.

After supper, they went to bed before their usual time. They wanted to get an early start the next morning.

Early Monday morning, on June 17, 1928, the Parker family left for Oklahoma. Ben hitched one team of horses to the wagon and led the other. The children were excited. They hadn't gone five miles until eight-year-old Earnest asked, "How long will it take us to get there?"

"About six days," Ben answered.

Eleven-year-old Artist said, "I want to go hunting and fishing with Francis."

"I'm sure he'll take you. He loves to hunt and fish."

Five-year-old Evelyn said, "I just want to play with my doll."

"There'll be plenty of time for playing," Ben answered.

Lavada began squirming and rubbing her eyes. At 23 months of age, she still needed naps during the daytime.

"Earnesteen, will you try and get Lavada to sleep?" Tildie asked. "Her eyes are drooping."

"Sure, I'll do it."

Ben and Tildie and their children continued along the road toward Oklahoma. They were also a little excited. This was their first trip of more than one day, and they were going to see their oldest son and their only grandson. They felt like pilgrims on a journey to a foreign land.

About noon the second day, they pulled into the town of Decatur. "Do you need any groceries?" Ben asked.

"No," Tildie answered. "I have enough for several days."

They found a shady spot just outside Decatur, stopped for dinner, then continued on their journey.

About 2:00 the third day, they crossed the Red River. The bridge over the Red River was a low-water bridge, but the river was down at that time of year, so the crossing was uneventful. They were now in Oklahoma. Everyone was keyed up, even Ben and Tildie. This was new country, even though it didn't look much different than the Texas plains they had just come through. They felt like they were in Francis's territory.

About 4:00 the fifth day, they were driving east on the road from Marlow. Ben wasn't sure what road he should take for Lindsay. There were several on the map, but which would be best? While he was pondering this question, they met a man on horseback going toward Marlow.

"Sir, which is the best way to get to Lindsay?" Ben asked.

"The easiest is to go east on this road for about 13 miles, then turn north. That road goes directly into Lindsay."

"My name is Ben Parker. This is my wife Tildie and these are our children."

"Pleased to meet you. I'm Duke Jackson. Are you visiting someone in Lindsay?"

"No, not in Lindsay. We're visiting our son. He lives about two or three miles south of Bradley."

"Your son wouldn't be Francis Parker?"

"That's him. We plan to visit with him a couple of weeks."

"I know Francis Parker. I've been a deputy sheriff in Grady County for 20 years. I met Francis last year while I was working on a case in Bradley."

"Small world, isn't it?"

"Yes, it is. I can tell you a shortcut to Francis's house that will save you at least 12 miles."

"I'd love that."

"You are now about three miles from Carin's Corner. You'll recognize it by a store on the north side called Carin's Grocery and Dry Goods.

Turn north just past the store. It's about five miles from there to Cox City. Just as you enter Cox City, you'll see the First Baptist Church on the left. Turn east just past the church. That road goes east about three miles, then dead-ends. Turn north and follow the main road to the Pikes Peak School. You'll have a few turns, but make sure you stay on the main road. A half-mile past Pikes Peak, the main road turns east. Don't turn. Keep going north. Francis's place is about three or four miles from there. His house sits to the west of the road about 100 yards, next to a hill with heavy timber."

"Thank you, so much. I sure appreciate the shortcut information."

"You're probably about ready to stop for the night. Less than a mile after you turn at Carin's Corner, you'll come to a creek with a nice, cool spring flowing from its bank. Pull down into the creek bed, and there's a good place to camp. From there, you can easily make Francis's place by 3:00 or 4:00 tomorrow. If you brought a gun, you can get some cottontails for supper. They're all over the place."

"No, we didn't bring a gun, but thanks for your information."

Excitement was mounting. They were less than a full day's drive from where Francis lived. The children had a grand time running and playing along the creek. Ben and Tildie both wore broad grins. They were going to see their oldest son for the first time in about four years. Anticipation could be read in their faces.

About 3:30 the next afternoon, they pulled into Francis's front yard. Francis and Dora came out to greet them. "Get down and come inside," Francis said. "You made good time. We didn't expect you until tomorrow."

"We met a man who gave us a shortcut," Ben answered.

"You must have come straight north from Pikes Peak."

"Yes, that's the way the man told us to come."

"No wonder you got here early," Francis said.

Ben looked toward the barn. "I need to unhitch the team."

"I'll do that, and put them in the barn," Francis said. "You go in the house and rest."

Roden and A T helped Francis unhitch the team. After feeding and watering them, they went into the house.

"Francis, when can we go fishing?" Artist asked.

"How about tomorrow?"

"Great. I'll be ready."

The next morning, Francis took Artist on a one-day fishing trip to the Washita River. Roden and A T went along, but it was obvious this trip was a special treat for Artist. He had a blast! He caught four bass and six catfish. "The bass are called largemouth and the catfish are called channel cats," Francis instructed.

When they got home, Artist couldn't wait to get his fish dressed and ready for the frying pan. "I almost beat Francis fishing," he told his mama. "He caught only one more than I did. I would have beat him if I hadn't let two fish get away."

That fishing trip invoked a competition between the two brothers that lasted for the rest of their lives. From then on, they were always trying to outdo one another either fishing or hunting.

The following morning, Francis asked, "Artist, would you like to go squirrel hunting? I know a good spot where we should be able to get several squirrels."

"I'd love it!" Artist answered. "Do you have an extra gun for me? We didn't bring one."

"I sure do," Francis replied. "Can you be ready in 30 minutes?"

"I'll be ready."

Although it wasn't in his nature to do so, and he never did it again, Francis let Artist get one more squirrel than he did. Artist was ecstatic. He had spent two glorious days with his oldest brother, fishing and hunting, and he even beat him the second day. He decided life was good at that point.

Ben and Tildie spent the next two weeks visiting with Francis and Dora, and playing with their grandson, Ollen, who was, at that time, seven months old. On Wednesday, June 26, the family had a small party to celebrate Lavada's second birthday.

Their time with Francis and Dora flew by. Too soon, Ben and his family were on their way back to Texas. Their joyful visit was over. The trip back was somber. It had been so pleasant visiting with their son, daughter-in-law and grandson.

About an hour after crossing the Red River into Texas, Ben spoke. "Tildie, I've noticed something. Did you see how much greener the crops were around Lindsay than they are here?"

"Yes, I did. Do you think we should move to Lindsay?"

"I think we should. My parents won't be around much longer and neither will your dad. We don't have much to keep us here now."

Tildie thought for a minute. "When we get home, let's write a letter to Francis. Maybe he can find us a sharecropper farm near him. If he can, I think we should move."

"Good idea. We'll do it."

At the crest of a hill about a half-mile before arriving at their house, Ben looked worried. "Tildie, there's something wrong. Our house looks strange. The shape is not right."

"You're right," Tildie answered. "I wonder what happened to it."

As they topped the next hill, the scene came into view. Almost half of the house was missing. Where the kitchen should be, there was a pile of burned rubble "Oh, no," Ben said. "We've had a fire."

"I wonder what happened," Tildie responded.

With somber faces, they got down from the wagon and began circling the house. In the kitchen area, there was a large mound of pot metal which had been Tildie's cookstove. Half-melted pots were lying nearby. Gnarled pieces of silverware and kitchen utensils lay scattered about. Ben had a hurt look, and Tildie bit her bottom lip so as to not frighten the children by showing too much emotion.

They left the kitchen area and walked around to the bedrooms. Soot was all over the roof and walls, but the bedrooms hadn't burned.

They circled around to the living room. It was about the same as the bedrooms. They opened the living room door and went in. The furniture in that room was missing. The only item left was the wood heater standing along the back wall. In the bedrooms, they found all the furniture left standing, but it was heat and smoke damaged. The nightstands were buckled, with black soot and smoke etched into the wood. Opening the closet doors, they found all the clothes and quilts stored there both smoke and heat damaged. None of it was usable.

"I wonder what happened to my trunk," Tildie remarked.

"I think someone got the trunk and living room furniture out," Ben answered.

Ben and Tildie were traumatized and the children seemed afraid. "What are we going to do?" Artist asked.

"Let's drive over to Poppa and Momma's house," Ben said. "Maybe they can tell us what happened."

In a few minutes, they pulled into Doc and Alice's front yard. Doc came out of the house. "Did you drive by your place?"

"Yes," Ben answered. "What happened?"

"Jerry White called and said your house was on fire. We rushed over there. Some of the neighbors helped, and we got most of the living room furniture out. We couldn't get to the other rooms. We got the fire put out before it burned the whole house down."

"How about my trunk?" Tildie asked.

"We got it out," Doc answered. "It's in the shed with the rest of the furniture."

"Thank goodness," Tildie said. "I had a lot of family heirlooms in it. I'm glad it didn't burn."

"The quilts that were on the beds are also in the shed," Alice said. "I hung them on the line to air out, just as you asked me to do. I got them off the line before much soot got on them."

"Thank you," Tildie answered. "At least we have some cover for next winter."

Doc took a deep breath. "Most of what was in the house is heat and smoke damaged. The only things you will be able to use are the bedsteads and heater. The rest is not usable."

Tildie frowned. "It's going to take a lot of money to replace it."

"You're going to need a place to stay," Doc said. "You can stay here with us until your landlord gets a new house built, or until you can find another one. The kids are gone, and we have plenty of room."

"Thanks," Ben answered. "That takes a load off my mind."

"I guess that means we don't have to replace our furniture right away," Tildie said.

Ben was silent for a few minutes, doing mental calculations. "I'm glad we've had a couple of good years. We have enough money in the bank to replace the furniture. That's a blessing."

"It sure is," Doc answered. "You're fortunate you won't have to borrow money to replace it."

The burned house was the clincher which caused Ben and Tildie to decide that a move to Oklahoma would be in their best interest. Texas would hold too many memories of their loss. In Oklahoma, they could truly start anew. It would be difficult leaving their friends around Brock, and the church they had attended together all their married life, but they could make new friends in Oklahoma. On many occasions during the rest of the summer, they discussed their plans to relocate in a new state. They loved the area around Lindsay and Bradley, and were anxious to move.

Over the summer, they communicated with Francis and Orville through letters. Near the middle of October, they sold their farming equipment and animals, planning to purchase what they needed in Oklahoma. Arrangements were made and, after the crops were gathered, Francis borrowed a truck and drove to Brock. Orville also came in his car, and the two of them moved the family to the See Chapel School District, south of Bradley.

This trip took five hours.

PROSPERITY

A 1929 Chevrolet Touring Car, like the one
Ben and Tildie bought that year

After the small recession in 1924, Ben and Tildie enjoyed four years of
prosperity in Texas. Farming was good and they got top prices when the
crops were sold. As a result, they had a fair-sized bank account. That was
a good thing. They needed the money they had saved to buy furniture
to replace that which was lost in the fire.

When the family arrived at Francis' place, he said, "I've found you
a sharecropper farm about a mile from here. There's also a farm auction
the other side of Bradley. It will be next Saturday. You can probably buy
everything you need, including furniture."

"Thank you, Francis. I'm anxious to get what we need," Ben
answered.

"You can stay here until Saturday. We'll have to make pallets on the
floor for the kids, but we can manage."

On Saturday, Ben, Tildie and Francis went to the auction. Ben was able to purchase his farming implements, furniture, horses and a milk cow and still leave a little in the bank. He and Tildie were happy. The future seemed bright.

The streak of prosperity begun in Texas in 1925 continued in Oklahoma. When spring arrived, Ben threw himself into the business of preparing the soil for planting crops. He used his turning plow, pulled by his new team of horses, to turn the weeds under on land which had lain fallow the previous year. As fresh soil was brought to the surface, he noticed how rich it was; not at all like the sandy soil around Brock. It was dark with sweet-smelling humus. *This should grow good crops*, he thought. He was filled with anticipation and new hope.

On Monday, March 11, 1929, Ben got a letter from Doc. In it, Doc said, "Your mother is very sick. It doesn't look like she will last more than a few days."

Ben looked at Tildie. "I think I should call Poppa. Francis' neighbor has a phone. I think I'll walk over there and call."

When Doc answered, Ben asked, "How's Momma?"

"Not good," Doc answered. "I don't think she'll last the night."

"I'll try to come to Brock," Ben said. "Maybe Francis can take me."

After hanging up the phone, Ben asked, "How much do you think a three-minute call to Brock, Texas will be?"

"About 50 cents," the neighbor answered.

"Here's 50 cents," Ben said. "If it is more, please let me know and I will pay the difference."

Ben walked to Francis' house. "Momma is in bad shape. Poppa doesn't think she will last until tomorrow."

"Would you like me to take you down there?" Francis asked.

"Yes, if you have time."

"I have time. I don't have anything I have to do until next week."

About an hour later, Francis, Ben and Tildie were on the way to Brock. When they got there, they found Ben's mother still alive but very weak. She passed away the next day, Tuesday, March 12, 1929. After the funeral, they returned to their homes in Oklahoma.

A couple of months later, on Saturday, May 13, Francis came to Ben and Tildie's house. "My neighbor took a call from Uncle Ed about an hour ago. He said Grandpa Parker died this morning. Do you want to go to Brock?"

"I'd like to," Ben answered.

Francis, Ben and Tildie made yet another trip to Texas for Doc's funeral. It was sad times, losing both of Ben's parents two months apart. While at Brock, they visited Tildie's father. "This may be the last time I get to see him," Tildie said.

Late in July, Ben finished the last cultivation on his June corn. As he entered the house, Tildie asked, "How are the crops?"

"Great," Ben answered. "The early corn and hygear are almost ready to harvest, and we have a good crop of both. I just laid by the June corn. The cotton is healthy and growing, putting on lots of blossoms. It looks like we will have a bumper crop of cotton."

Near the end of October, Ben came in from a trip to Lindsay. "Tildie, I think it's time we got our own car."

"What do you mean?"

"I sold the last of our crops. We had a good cotton crop and I got $360.00 a ton for it. We now have $1,300.00 in the bank. I saw a brand new 1929 Chevrolet touring car in Lindsay. We can buy it for $645.00.

Let's get it. We could pay cash for it. That would leave $655.00 in the bank for a nest egg. We wouldn't have to depend on Francis to take us where we need to go."

Tildie was thoughtful for a minute. "Why don't we buy it on the credit plan? We could pay $200.00 down and leave an even larger nest egg. We could make the payments from our bank account and replace the money as we sell crops. How much would the payments be?"

Ben mentally calculated the payment. "About $19.50 a month. I also think we should take out a life insurance policy on me. That way, if anything happened to me, you would be well cared for, at least until the children are grown. We can get a $10,000.00 policy for $50.00 down and $15.00 a quarter."

"Okay. Why don't you make arrangements for both? I would also like a new pressure canner. The one I'm using is a hand-me-down from Mother, and it's about worn out. I could also use a new sewing machine."

"I'll take care of it tomorrow."

Ben purchased the car, the sewing machine and pressure canner Tildie wanted, and the life insurance policy. When he got home, the family piled into the new car, and they went to Francis and Dora's house, to show it off. In a few minutes, they drove into Francis' yard. "Woo, wee," Francis said. "That sure is a nice car."

"Thank you," Ben answered. "I just bought it about an hour ago, at the Chevrolet Garage in Lindsay."

On Saturday, November 16, 1929, Francis again came to Ben and Tildie's house with bad news. "Grandpa Bratcher passed away this morning. Dollie called my neighbor to let us know."

"We can take our own car this time," Ben said. "But, if you want to go, I'd love to have you drive it."

TRIALS

Reading the Bible in the Barn
During the trying times of the Great Depression, Dan often
studied and prayed in an empty stall in the barn.

After returning from Sandy Bratcher's funeral, Ben and Tildie began counting their blessings. They had a new car, a life insurance policy, everything they needed for their farming operations, $1,000.00 in the bank and enough cash to last them through the winter. However, they were not aware that the ominous winds of change were already blowing.

On Sunday, December 29, 1929, in his State of the Union address, President Hoover announced the stock market crash, which had occurred on October 29 of that year. All across the nation, people were glued to their radio, anxiously listening for any breaking news about the stock market. Ben and his family were no exception. Even though they didn't have any investments in stocks, they listened to every newscast. They were aware that the crash could place them in a precarious situation. "I'm glad we have a nest egg," Ben said.

Two days later, on Tuesday, December 31, another momentous event occurred. Oklahoma received a massive snowstorm. It came barreling down from the northwest, along with strong winds. The snow fell wet and heavy, drifting in front of the cold norther. Within 24 hours, drifts of ten or more feet were common in sheltered places, and the snow was as much as six feet deep in more open country. After the snowstorm ended, the temperature plummeted to near zero, and the very wet snow froze into a solid mass of white ice.

At supper, Tildie announced, "We're almost out of basic groceries."

"We're almost out of oats and mash for the livestock," Ben said. "We're also almost out of wood for the stoves. I need to go to Lindsay tomorrow to get supplies. Roden, could you and A T cut some wood while I'm gone?"

"Yes, we will," Roden answered.

"I'll help them," Artist said.

"Will you take the car?" Tildie asked.

"No. I'm afraid it will get stuck in the snow. If that happens, it'll be there until spring. I'll take a team of horses and the wagon. If it gets stuck, I can come back for another team to pull it out."

On Thursday morning, Ben hitched his best team of horses to the wagon. On the way out of their yard, he had a thought. If he headed east and varied north a small amount, he could be at the Washita River Bridge in three miles, instead of the seven miles it would take him following the road through Bradley. With luck, he could drive right over the tops of the fences that surrounded the farms in the area. It worked. Even the five-wire fences were completely covered by the snow. His trip to Lindsay was five miles, not the nine miles it would take using the road.

When Ben returned, Tildie said, "That didn't take near as long as I thought it would."

"I drove right through our neighbor's fields, straight to the river bridge."

"What did you do about the fences?"

"The snow had the fences covered and was frozen solid. It was a breeze."

"You never could have done that with the car."

"I don't think so. The weight would probably cause the car to break through the snow."

The great snowstorm actually was a blessing in disguise. It melted slowly and raised the water table over most of the state. As a result, most farmers in Oklahoma were better able to feed their families during the trying times of the Great Depression.

For a few months after the snowstorm, Ben and his family enjoyed some good times. They had a nice bank account and were making the payments on their car and insurance policy. Life was good again. They visited often with Francis, Dora and their grandson, Ollen. They were both happy and contented in Oklahoma.

Then, in April of 1930, tragedy struck again. Little three-year old Lavada suddenly became ill with a fever. Her little body quickly began wasting away. In about a week, she became "skin and bones" as the saying goes. Then her fever increased.

Francis drove into Lindsay to get Doctor Hugh Monroe. He examined her and said, "She's got diphtheria. There isn't much chance she will make it. Her fever is 105 degrees. She can't live long under those conditions."

"How did she get it?" Tildie asked.

"What's your water supply?" Doctor Monroe questioned.

"Right now, we're drinking spring water. We don't have a well yet."

"That's most likely where she got it."

Ben and Tildie knew the power of prayer. They petitioned God earnestly. "Please, God, You can heal our little girl. Please heal her, if it is Your will to do so. If not, we are subject to Your will."

Lavada's fever hovered around 105 degrees for three days. Then it broke, but it had damaged her brain. She was no longer the bright, intelligent child she was before her illness. She had to learn to talk and walk all over again, and could not learn anything as well as other children her age.

"We can deal with her condition," Ben said. "I'm just glad we have our little girl back."

About two months after Lavada's bout with diphtheria, on June 17, 1930, President Hoover signed the Hawley-Smoot Tariff Bill into law. Some historians believe this bill caused the Depression to worsen. Trade with foreign countries quickly reduced to a trickle. Farmers had no place to sell their crops except the domestic market. The prices they got for their wares were pitifully low. Banks began closing their doors and going into bankruptcy.

A few weeks after President Hoover signed the bill, Ben saw one of his neighbors, James Sinclair, at church. "Have you heard that a couple of the banks in Lindsay have closed?" James asked.

"No, I haven't," Ben answered. "Has the Lindsay Farmer's Bank closed?"

"Not yet. At least not that I'm aware of."

When Ben and his family got home, he and Tildie discussed what James had said. "Maybe you should go to Lindsay tomorrow and take our money out of the bank," Tildie suggested.

"I was thinking the same thing. I'll drive over tomorrow and do that."

When Ben returned from town the next afternoon, he had a dejected look. "It's too late. Our bank has already closed. It had a sign in the window which read, 'Closed due to bankruptcy procedure.'"

"Do you think God is punishing us because we moved from Texas?" Tildie asked.

"No. There are millions of people in the same boat we're in. God would be unjust if He punished millions of people just to punish us."

"What are we going to do? We can't pay for the car on the amount of money crops and livestock are selling for now."

"We'll just have to let it be repossessed. We can barely feed our family now. A car is a luxury we can do without. The same goes for the life insurance policy."

Tildie was sad, but there was no other choice. The family came first. Luxuries were no longer important.

STRUGGLES

A Go-devil Frame
To be of use in cultivating crops, this frame would be
mounted on a pair of sled runners made from two-by-
six inch lumber, with a metal strip along the bottom.
(The 2X6 wooden runners have rotted off)

Ben and Tildie entered a new phase in their lives. They now had no transportation other than a wagon pulled by a team of horses. They went to church whenever they could, but mostly they just stayed home and worshiped God in their own way. They read their Bibles and prayed daily. They also said grace at every meal and had family prayer at bedtime.

Their daily devotions were unique. Sometimes they had their supplications together, but most of the time they each prayed and read scripture in their own way. Tildie usually sat down with some daily task, such as shelling black-eyed peas, snapping green beans or churning butter. While doing these chores, she read her Bible and prayed.

Ben usually took his Bible to the barn and sat on a bale of hay while doing devotions. Ben often said, "I don't want to talk to God. I want to talk with God. If I don't listen to Him, I might as well write my requests on a piece of paper, lay them in front of me and say, 'There's my list, Lord. You can read it as well as I can.' That's the reason I read my Bible while praying. It tells me what God wants from me."

On Sunday, September 28, 1930, their tenth child was born, a boy. Tildie had served as a midwife in Texas, but she had not yet established that precedent in their community in Oklahoma. She didn't know anyone who was serving as a midwife, so she wanted a doctor to deliver her baby. Ben went to a neighbor who had a phone and called Doctor Hugh Monroe.

After the delivery, Doctor Monroe asked, "Do you have a name for your new son?"

"We have a first name," Tildie answered. "It's Loran."

"I don't have any children, and no one to be named after me. How about Hugh for a middle name? I'd buy his christening outfit if you would name him Hugh."

"That's as good a name as any. How about it, Ben?"

"That would be okay by me."

The birth certificate for their tenth child read Loran Hugh Parker.

Even though it was a struggle, Ben and Tildie managed to keep food on the table for their eight children still at home. Theirs was a happy family. Francis came by often to visit. Gertrude and her husband, Orville, came when they could. They both obtained minister's licenses with the Church of God, with headquarters in Cleveland, Tennessee. Orville served as pastor of a Church of God in Texas. Gertrude served as his associate, and preached when he had to be away on church business. About the only time they had to visit was for short periods of time during the week. They were too busy on the weekends.

The year 1931 arrived with no letup in sight for the devastating effects of the Depression. Wages were still going down. Farm labor, which paid 25¢ an hour in 1929, now paid 10¢. It was difficult to sell crops and livestock. The price of hogs plummeted from 42¢ a pound to 4¢. The situation was made worse by the fact that the price farmers had to pay for necessities didn't fall as much as the price they were being paid for their crops and livestock.

During that year, on Saturday, August 15, Roden Franklin Parker married Leola Wilkins. Then, on Thursday, December 17, A T Parker married Leola's older sister, Martha Jewel Wilkins. Roden and Leola moved to a sharecropper farm about five miles south of Ben and Tildie's place and began their new life in a two-room log cabin. A T and Martha moved to Eastern Oklahoma.

The days and months rolled by, like a wheel turning in slow motion. Wages for farm labor hit an all-time low in 1932: 5¢ an hour. A person needed to work three hours to buy a hamburger and a drink. It took 10 hours of work to buy an everyday pair of overalls. Ben and Tildie bought few new clothes for their family. Instead, Tildie patched and re-patched their clothing, making them last as long as she could. Almost all they ate or used came from their farm. They sold whatever they could do without and made do with what they had.

In the fall of 1933, Francis and Dora moved to a larger sharecropper farm about a mile from where Roden and Leola lived. That left Ben and Tildie effectively alone. It was an all day trip in a wagon to visit with Roden or Francis, even for a few hours. They couldn't afford the time. All their energies were used to keep food on the table for their six children left at home.

On Friday, May 18, 1934, the eleventh and last child arrived, a girl whom they named Theta Mae. The care of the new baby, as well as the housework, was shared by Tildie, Earnesteen and Evelyn. Ben, Artist and Earnest shared the farming operations. Everyone worked, and all were happy. They learned from Tildie and Ben that a cheerful family life is the most important part of living.

As the end of the year neared, Ben became restless. He missed having Francis close by. He missed the frequent visits they had enjoyed for three years. At supper one evening, he said, "Tildie, I've found a sharecropper farm around the corner from the Oak Grove School. It is larger than this one, and has a four-room house. We can farm it for 25% of the crops. We're now paying 30%, so we should be able to do better there. Also, it is only about three miles from where Roden lives, and four miles from Francis. We could visit them more often."

"If you'll be happier there, take it. I'll be happy wherever we are."

"I'll contact the owner tomorrow and tell him we'll take it."

About the middle of November, Ben borrowed a wagon and a team of horses from Roden. He and his family loaded their belongings on the two wagons and moved to the Oak Grove School district. The weather was cold, so four-year old Loran and six-month old Theta were placed between two feather mattresses to keep them warm. Everyone else wore heavy coats. Some of the family members even walked alongside the wagons to keep warm.

Their new home was situated a quarter-mile southeast of the Oak Grove schoolhouse. The next day after moving in, Ben and Tildie took Evelyn and Lavada to school. It was a two-room affair, much the same as every other rural Oklahoma school of that time. Ben requested to meet with the principal, Mr. Janzen.

"Lavada had diphtheria at age three," he explained. "It left her with brain damage. She will probably have trouble keeping up with the first graders."

"Mrs. Janzen is teaching the lower grades. She will help Lavada in every way possible."

"Evelyn will help her, too. I just wanted you to know the situation."

Not long after moving to Oak Grove, Earnesteen met Joe Isaiah Mauldin. They began dating, and it wasn't long until most of the family became aware that they would probably get married.

In the summer of 1935, Earnest found a job that paid 15¢ an hour. He worked all summer and saved most of what he made. Then, he found a used Chevrolet Roadster with a rumble seat. The owner was eager to sell, so Earnest bought it. He hadn't been driving very long, and had no experience driving on dirt roads, so he was a little reckless, a habit he easily overcame once he saw what reckless driving could do.

"Come go for a ride in my new car," Earnest said.

The family eagerly piled in. The one inside seat and the rumble seat quickly filled up. Earnesteen and Joe rode on the running boards, Earnesteen on the driver's side and Joe on the passenger's side. They held hands across the top of the car.

"You're driving too fast," Tildie cautioned.

"I'm okay," Earnest said.

About that time, he took a left corner too fast. The car began skidding toward the bar ditch. Joe jumped off and rolled into the ditch. The car skidded into the waterway a little further on, turned up on the passenger's side and dropped back on all four wheels.

Everyone survived this small wreck with only slight bruises and cuts, and Earnest learned a valuable lesson. Never again would he drive in a reckless manner.

Ben and his family had lived at Oak Grove almost a year when school started near the middle of August, 1935. Although Loran was ready and anxious to start school, Oklahoma law stated that a student must be five years old on the first day of school in order to be enrolled in the Primary grade. Loran was about one month too young, so he had to stay home one more year.

The next spring, on Easter Sunday, April 12, 1936, Earnesteen and Joe married. When the crops were gathered that fall, they moved—first to Arizona, then to California to continue their new life together. They didn't wait for Evelyn and Lavada to come home from school to say goodbye. They were in a hurry to get to their new home, so they just left. Joe's cousin and his wife went with them in Joe's roadster coup with a rumble seat. His cousin's wife had a baby in arms and was expecting their second child. Since she needed to ride inside the car, Earnesteen and Joe's cousin rode in the rumble seat all the way to Arizona.

Most row crops Ben grew were planted in furrows about twelve inches deep, eight inches wide and about eighteen inches apart. The furrows were made using a lister pulled by a team of horses. After the crop being grown was several inches high, he began the cultivation. The first two cultivations were done using a go-devil. That was a farm implement used at that time which consisted of a small sled which was eight inches wide, with a seat to ride on, and a set of disks on either side at the rear. The disks pulled dirt into the furrow, covering weeds and grass but leaving the crop being grown extending above the dirt. The go-devil was pulled by a team of horses.

Ben had a rather large field of corn to be cultivated and not much time to get it done. Artist had moved back to Texas, and Earnest had signed up for a one-year stint with the Civilian Conservation Corp. Loran was the only boy left at home, and he was a mere five years old.

"Do you think you could drive a team of horses?" Ben asked.

"Sure, I can."

"Okay. I'll borrow a go-devil and a team of horses from Roden. I want you to help me cultivate our corn field."

Ben hitched a team of horses to each go-devil and placed each in a furrow. He had Loran get on one and he got on the other.

"Giddyup," Ben and Loran said in unison.

The two teams pulled their implements to the end of the row, and both said, "Whoa."

Ben turned his go-devil around, then turned Loran's around. The procedure was repeated, and the two of them cultivated the field of corn in much less time than it would have required Ben to do so alone. Loran was very proud of the fact that he helped his papa cultivate corn that spring.

Near the middle of August in 1936, Loran started in the Primary grade at the Oak Grove School. About a month later, during their supper, Ben said, "I've got bad news. The owner of this farm wants us to move. He's going to farm it himself."

"Isn't it a little late for him to tell us?" Tildie asked.

"Yes it is, but we have no other choice. I'll have to scramble to find another farm. Maybe Roden and Francis can help."

A few days later, Roden came to their house. "I've found a small sharecropper farm about three-quarters of a mile from the Pikes Peak

School. It's the only one I could find. It may not grow enough for your needs, but I can help if it doesn't supply enough."

"All right. We'll move there," Ben said.

"In late November, the family moved to the farm Roden had found. Again, it was cold and they had to bundle up in order to keep warm. When they got there, they discovered that the small, two-room house hadn't been lived in for a few years. Dust was everywhere. Tildie's broom was worn out, so she had thrown it away. The house needed the attention of a good broom.

"Ben, I saw some broomweed down by the barn. Could you gather several stalks for me?"

"I sure can."

While Ben went for the broomweed, Tildie found a stick about four feet long, and some baling wire. When he returned, she bundled the weeds around the end of the stick and tied it with the wire. It made a crude, but effective broom.

"Where did you learn to do that?"

"From Old Indian Joe. He said his ancestors didn't use anything else for sweeping."

Christmas that year was somewhat different. Ben and Tildie had saved a little money from the previous farm. Ordinarily, Christmas gifts consisted of shirts for the boys and blouses, skirts or bloomers for the girls, all hand-made by Tildie and fashioned from printed flour or feed sacks. That year, there were store-bought presents for all the children. Evelyn got a new make-up kit. Lavada and Theta each got a doll. Loran got a new toy truck, complete with headlights operated by flashlight batteries. Six-year-old Loran was up first, and found his truck under the Christmas tree, even though daylight hadn't completely arrived. Theta came to the tree next, but it was too dark for her to find her doll. Loran turned on the headlights of his new truck to light the way.

That farm didn't supply enough. Ben often walked, or took the wagon to Lindsay and did odd jobs to earn extra money. It was needed to buy the items their small farm didn't supply. One day, as Ben was driving his team of horses and wagon back home after doing a job, he was stopped by a small band of gypsies in a Ford Roadster. Not wanting to appear unfriendly, Ben got down from the wagon.

"My name is Don Barrow," one of the men said.

"Pleased to meet you. I'm Ben Parker."

"Mr. Parker, do you have a match. I need one for a smoke and I'm out."

"I don't think so."

Ben put his hands in his pockets to check for the possibility that he had one he didn't know about. One of the women grabbed him from behind, pinning his arms to his sides. The man went through his pockets. All they got was the 50¢ he had just been paid for the job he did in town. It was all the money he had.

After the anger of being robbed faded away, Ben laughed about it. "I guess they needed that 50¢ more than I did."

That summer, Earnest came home from the Civilian Conservation Corp. He had spent his one-year with the CCC at a camp in the Sierra Nevada Mountains of California, clearing timber and building roads. As a result, he had grown muscular and strong.

Ben had a heifer he was trying to break to milk. He wasn't having any luck. The young cow would kick, often knocking the bucket out of his hand, spilling the milk. "Let me milk her," Earnest said.

When Earnest began milking, she kicked at the bucket. Earnest grabbed her foot, placed his shoulder in her flank and flipped her over onto her back. She never kicked again, and eventually made one of the best milk cows Ben ever had.

In a few weeks, Earnest found a small farm and moved out. His stint with the CCC had changed him to an independent individual. He could take care of himself.

Ben began looking for a larger sharecropper farm in the area. He found one which was about twice the size of the present farm, and made arrangements to move there after the crops were harvested. It was about 80 acres, all farming land. He made arrangements with the owner of a large wooded pasture to graze his horses and cattle there. He also got permission to cut firewood from the abundance of post oak and blackjack trees it contained.

The farm was located one-half mile north and one and three-fourths miles west of the Pikes Peak School. In November, 1937, they moved to the new location. It had a two-room house, much like the other sharecropper farms in the area. As an added feature, there was a large screened-in porch on the north side. Tildie obtained some isinglass to cover the screen. Isinglass was made by impregnating a thin, flexible screen wire with a gelatin made from the air bladder of various fishes. It was a precursor to plastic. The isinglass was rolled up in the summer, and let down in the winter.

Seven-year old Loran quickly got a lesson in keeping warm at night. That porch became his bedroom. It had no heat, so he learned how to slide under the cold covers and get warm in a hurry. He would lie on his back on the bottom sheet, place the pillows on each side of his head and pull the covers up to his chin. The only part of his body not covered would be his face. In a few minutes, he would be warm as toast. He would then place one of the pillows under his head and go to sleep. In the wintertime, he often woke up in the morning with snow scattered over his bed. The wind had blown the snow through the cracks where the isinglass was overlapped.

That house didn't have a cooler box, as did the other sharecropper houses. Ben made one and placed it on the north side of the house. He fashioned a wooden frame three feet on all sides. He built a wooden bottom and top, and covered the sides with heavy ducking. The cloth was kept wet during warm weather. The evaporation of the water kept the inside cool. Perishable food was stored in the cooling box.

The dust bowl in the Oklahoma Panhandle had peaked during the winter of 1936. Even so, great clouds of dust were still blowing along the northern border of Oklahoma during the fall and winter of 1937. Some reports say the grimy silt from the Dust Bowl blew all the way to the East Coast and out into the Atlantic. The house for the farm where Ben and his family were now living was at the crest of a small hill. From there, they could see the dust clouds.

Tildie once remarked, "I don't see how the people living in the Panhandle can stand all that dust."

Actually, very few people were left in the Panhandle at that time. In 1936, they had reached the limit of their endurance and just moved away, most of them to California. Most families loaded what personal belongings they could haul in their car and left the rest of their possessions. They usually made their last stop for gas either at Gorman or Boise City, then drove away.

There were many and varied reasons for the Dust Bowl. However, there were two main causes. First, too much of the prairie grasses had been plowed under in order for the farmers to plant wheat. Second, the area was usually watered by gentle, moist south winds from the Gulf of Mexico. In the winter of 1930, dry winds began blowing over the Rocky Mountains from the north-west. They collided with the south winds and turned them to the north-east. These contrary winds continued throughout the decade of the 1930s, subsiding in 1939. Under those conditions, there was nothing the land could do but dry up.

Just after moving to that house, the Parkers saw another phenomenon which they had never seen before, and never saw again. The aurora borealis could be seen from their farm. On several occasions, they observed the northern lights dancing near the horizon. The undulating glow would change from reddish to bluish, play in the night sky for perhaps fifteen minutes to an hour, then fade away. Sometimes they would return within an hour, or the next night, or stay away for several weeks.

"I wonder why we can see the northern lights from here." Tildie said.

"My guess is that the static electricity produced by the dry wind and the dust attracted the aurora borealis and pulled it further to the south than it normally would be," Ben answered.

The diminutive crops grown on their previous farm caught up with them the next spring. On two separate occasions, they ran out of basic food items. For two or three days at a time, until Ben could get to town and sell something, the only food for the family to eat was cornmeal mush and milk. Even though the same food for several days became boring and monotonous, they thanked God for what they had. At least, the family didn't have to go hungry.

PEACEMAKING

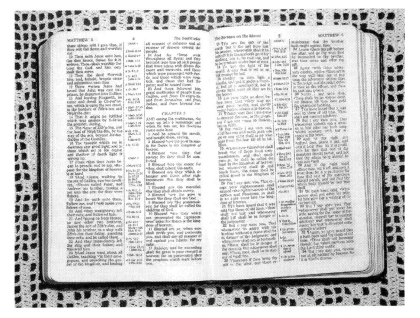

Matthew 5:9
Blessed are the peacemakers . . .

Near the middle of March, 1937, Artist came home for a short time. He had been living in Texas a little more than a year, and his family was glad to see him.

"Mama and Papa, I need to talk to you," Artist said. "I've been dating Thelma Tillery. You know Thelma, don't you?"

"She has a bad reputation," Tildie answered.

"I know, but it's undeserved. She's really a sweet, loving girl; not at all like the rumors people have circulated about her. We want to get married. The only way she will marry me is for you to give your blessings."

Ben remembered Thelma from his dealings with her family when he and Tildie lived in Texas. Although still a child at the time, she was a tomboy. She could whip any boy in the area where they lived and wasn't afraid to rough-house with them. As she progressed into her teen years, her boyish ways earned her the title of a loose girl. Ben knew that wasn't a valid reason to brand her an unsuitable bride.

"I don't judge a person by their reputation," Ben said. "I judge them by their present lifestyle. As far as I can tell, Thelma would make you a good wife. You have my blessings."

"Mine, too," Tildie responded.

Ben was silent for a few seconds. "There's one problem. We're too busy getting our crops planted to attend a wedding. Our food supply is low, and we need to get something growing."

"That's okay," Artist responded. "Francis said he'll take me back to Texas and be my best man."

Artist and Thelma were married on March 20. The only members of his family at the wedding were Francis and Dora, along with their three children.

Emily Dickinson wrote a short, untitled poem that effectively stated Ben's philosophy:

> If I can stop one heart from breaking,
> I shall not live in vain;
> If I can ease one life the aching,
> Or cool one pain,
> Or help one fainting robin
> Into his nest again,
> I shall not live in vain.

A few weeks after Artist and Thelma's wedding, Ben was talking with P. H. Gregg, his neighbor to the south.

"I met a lady in Lindsay a few days ago," Ben began. "She said you're her brother."

"That would be Louise Hicks," P. H. answered. "She's my sister, but we don't speak to each other."

"Would you mind telling me why?"

"I drink too much, and we had a falling out about that. We don't see eye-to-eye."

"I get the feeling she would like to change that," Ben responded. "Would you talk to her if I would be your mediator?"

P. H. was silent for a few moments. "I don't know. Why don't you check with her? She lives about three-quarters of a mile straight north of you. Let me know what she says."

A few days later, Ben walked to the Hicks' house. "Louise, would you be willing to try and settle your differences between you and your brother?" Ben asked.

"I would be if he's willing," Louise answered.

"He seems to be," Ben said. "He wanted to hear what you have to say before committing himself."

Louise hesitated a moment. "You seem to be a good man. Would you act as our go-between?"

"I would love to," Ben answered.

Ben arranged for the two families to meet the next Monday. When the day arrived, the Parker family had supper about an hour earlier than usual. A few minutes after the dishes were finished, the Gregg family came walking up the dirt driveway. Ben said, "We're going somewhere tonight with the Greggs."

Ben got two flashlights and handed one to Tildie. "We'll be coming home after dark. We'll need these."

When the two families arrived at the Hicks', the children of all three families were instructed to stay outside and play. The adults went into the house. The tension was so thick between the Greggs and the Hicks you could cut it with a knife. P. H. and Louise mostly refrained from looking at each other. When they did, you could see the suspicion in their eyes.

Ben began. "Louise and P. H., both of you have agreed to meet and try to work out your differences. If either of you feels you can't go on, please say so. We can stop this meeting at any time. As long as both of you agree that progress is being made, we can continue. You both need to bring your hurt feelings out into the open. You need to ask for and give forgiveness for any wrong done. Why don't we start? P. H., why don't you go first?"

"We just don't see eye-to-eye," P. H. answered.

"I know, but what specific hurt do you have?" Ben questioned.

"She called me a drunk."

"Direct that statement to Louise."

P. H. looked at Louise. "I got hurt when you called me a drunk."

Louise bit her lip. "I shouldn't have, but you do drink too much."

P. H. ducked his head. "I know that. I've tried to quit, but I can't."

"It's almost impossible to quit on your own," Ben said. "It's an addiction. The only people I know who have quit did so by becoming a Christian and allowing God and the church people to help them."

"Louise, what hurts do you have?" Ben asked.

With an offended look, Louise answered, "P. H., you called me a meddling bitch."

"I shouldn't have," P. H. responded. "Would you forgive me?"

Louise's eyes suddenly sparkled. "Yes. Would you forgive me for calling you a drunk?"

"Yes, I will."

P. H. and Louise embraced. They smiled for the first time since the meeting started. Tears filled both their eyes.

"Are these all the hurts?" Ben asked.

"No," P. H. answered.

"Let's work through them one at a time," Ben counseled. "We're making progress. If you need me, I'll stay with you all night."

It was well after dark when the two families walked back in silence along the path to Ben and Tildie's house. "Thank you, Ben," P. H. said. "I feel like a heavy weight has been lifted from my shoulders."

"Blessed are the peacemakers, for they shall be called sons of God." Matthew 5:9.

Ben didn't feel like a peacemaker. He felt like a neighbor helping a fellow neighbor. After they went to bed that night, he said, "Tildie, please don't tell the children what happened tonight." He didn't want his children to think of him as a spiritual giant. He just wanted to be their Papa.

Tildie kept that promise for the next 10 years; then she told Loran what transpired at the Hicks' house.

The peacemaking Ben instituted that night worked. Over the next few years, each of the two families was observed on several occasions walking along the footpath to visit the other family. They were friendly with each other from that point on.

It's not that these two families were "pillars" of the community. The Hicks were not very well known to Ben and his family, but the Greggs were another matter. Loran and Theta went to school with the Gregg children, and came to know them quite well. They had two boys and one girl.

P. H. was drunk much of the time. Even though the Depression was still in full swing, and money was extremely scarce, he would drink up almost all the cash he could get his hands on. In addition, he was ornery and often downright mean. His wife, Lillie, was the only bright spot in the family. She was a kind, hard-working woman, who tried to be a good neighbor. The two boys were like their dad, and the younger one was a bully. The daughter was sometimes like her mom, and sometimes like her dad.

Most people would say, "It's not worth the effort to get those two families to reconcile their differences."

Ben didn't think that way. His and Tildie's kindness and consideration for others were very well demonstrated that night. They both considered it an honor to help those two families.

THE BRUSH ARBOR

A Brush Arbor

During the first part of the twentieth century, and especially during the Great Depression, the brush arbor was an important entity in spreading the gospel of Jesus Christ. It was usually constructed after the farmers in a particular area had laid their crops by, and before harvest time began. That time frame usually fell somewhere between the middle of June to the middle of August. A resident or itinerate preacher would contact a local farmer or rancher and get permission to construct a brush arbor on his place. Sometimes the owner of the farm would help with the construction.

Brush arbors were first built during pioneer days in North Central Louisiana. They were used as temporary shelters while the occupants were clearing land and building permanent dwellings. When the need for spiritual enlightenment was deemed necessary, they were converted to outdoor churches.

The arbor was usually laid out to be about 20 by 30 feet. A row of posts, of sufficient height to place the roof about ten feet above the ground, were placed along each side and sometimes down the middle. The roof was built with a slight pitch, to allow any rain to drain off. The roof was made using small branches of any trees which were available. In Ben's area, that was usually post oak or white oak, as they had leaves large enough to shed the rain.

Benches for the parishioners were constructed using stumps about 16 inches high with a two by twelve piece of lumber nailed or laid on top of the stumps. The pulpit was often a large post set in the ground near the head of the arbor, and standing about four feet high. A short section of two by twelve lumber was nailed to the top of the post to form a flat surface for the preacher to place his Bible and notes, and for him to pound his fist to make a point.

For evening services, the only light source was a pump-type kerosene lantern, solely for the benefit of the preacher. Since a good pumping of the light would last about two hours, the preacher would know it was time to stop when the flame began to flicker and grow dim. Sometimes the mischievous boys in the congregation would volunteer to pump up the lantern prior to the service. They would intentionally not pump it up all the way, so the service would be shorter.

At the end of the service, the congregation would light their own lanterns for the trip home.

Just after July 4, 1938, Ben heard of a brush arbor being built on the road to Lindsay, about four miles from their house. He checked with the owner of the land and was told an itinerate preacher was scheduled to hold an eight-day revival under the bower, beginning the next Sunday. Returning home, he said, "Tildie, there's a brush arbor revival a mile east of the Hanley corner, starting Sunday. I think we should go to it."

"How long will it last?" Tildie asked.

"Eight days. From Sunday to Sunday."

"We can manage that. The children are out of school, and won't need to get up so early. Let's go."

During the next week, the Parker family did their chores early and ate supper before dark. It took about 45 minutes to drive a team of horses the four miles to the meeting. Services started at 8:00, so they needed to be through with their evening meal and dressed, ready to go, a few minutes after 7:00. Each evening that week, Ben and Tildie herded their four children left at home into their wagon and went to the revival.

As was usually the case in a brush arbor meeting, the sermons were evangelistic in nature. The minister gave an altar call at the end of each service, for people to accept Jesus as their personal savior, and usually someone responded. On the fourth night, Evelyn, age 15, went to the altar. She had received Jesus as her savior the preceding year during one of the family devotions, but she wanted to make it public, so she responded to the call.

After the revival was over, Ben and Tildie discussed the outcome. "I'm glad Evelyn went to the altar," Tildie said. "I know she was saved last year, but now everyone else in the community knows it, too."

"That's true," Ben answered.

"I would have liked for some of the other children to respond," Tildie said.

"Don't worry about it," Ben replied. "None of the other three have reached the age of accountability. I believe they'll respond when the time comes."

As it turned out, that was the last brush arbor revival the Parker family attended. They were, even then, on the wane. Small rural congregations had already begun holding their meetings in local schoolhouses.

The need for brush arbors was almost over.

WHAT BEN TAUGHT

Shocks of hygear drying in the sun

The character, morals and values of most people are a direct result of what they learned from their parents. Ben and Tildie taught their children valuable lessons that served them well in later years.

Tildie openly instructed their children, boys and girls alike, the fine art of cooking, sewing and housekeeping. The boys often complained, "That's girl's work."

"You'll thank me later," she said. "When your wife becomes sick and can't do this work, at least you won't starve or live in a messy house."

It was different with Ben. Sometimes he used words, but mostly he modeled what he wanted to teach. He had several proverbs for different occasions. Sometimes he taught with his one-line sayings, such as:

"If you don't have enough brawn, use your brain."

When Ben used this saying, he was usually encouraging his children to look for easier ways to do things that gave them trouble. As a result, they grew up knowing they could find easier ways to perform difficult tasks.

"The first one can come anytime. All the rest take nine months."

Ben often used this saying when a newly married couple had their first child before they were married nine months. He was not judgmental, and would never condemn a young couple for getting pregnant before the wedding. He believed that past mistakes were much less important than the present and the future. What a person did with their life now was much more important than their past. To him, previous mistakes were to be forgiven and forgotten. What a person is now defines the person.

"There are lots of ways to skin a cat and not have it scratch you."

This saying was heard many times by his offspring. In his own unique way, he was telling them to look for a better way of performing the task at hand. Having many more years of wisdom, he was encouraging them to do the job at hand in a more efficient manner. He was a very smart man, and knew many ways to perform almost any task he had to do on the farm.

Ben also taught during the process of daily living. His lessons were learned and remembered by his children. In the process of daily living, without words, he taught them to:

Make hay while the sun shines.

Although they didn't often "make hay" as such, the principle was there. They grew a crop which was called hygear. It was a food plant for livestock, much like milo or cafricorn, except taller and more palatable. It was cut by hand with a knife similar to a machete, bundled, tied with a string and stacked in "shocks" of about twenty-five bundles. Each shock looked much like a small Indian teepee. I'm sure most people have seen pictures of the old Western United States in the autumn, with fields of shocked fodder and possibly a few pumpkins scattered throughout the field. The poem "When the Frost is on the Punkin'," by James Whitcomb Riley, is a word picture based on just such a scene.

If the hygear is cut while wet, then placed in shocks, it will mold and be worthless for livestock food. It was always harvested on a sunny day. After being shocked, it repelled rain naturally. During a storm, the outer layer was the only part that would get wet, and it would quickly dry when the rain stopped.

Also, fields were never plowed during or immediately after a rain, as the ground would be too wet, causing the soil to compact into a hard mass.

Do maintenance on a rainy day.

While it was raining, Ben mended the harness used on the horses, put half soles on shoes that still had good upper parts, did repairs to the inside of the house or barn, and any other maintenance that could be done indoors. When the sun was shining, he was too busy with other farm chores to do upkeep. That work was always saved for a rainy day.

Keep machinery cleaned and maintained.

Ben taught his children to be sure farm equipment was cleaned and in good repair before putting it away. If a plow was put away with dirt on it, the moisture from the soil caused it to rust. When the plow was next used, the rust reduced its efficiency. Until the rust wore off, it would not "throw" the dirt as it should, and was more difficult for the horses to pull, thus causing them to tire earlier. When a wheel was not properly greased, not only would the wheel or axle wear out faster, it was more difficult for the horses to pull. For these reasons, the wagon wheels were greased often, and Ben would not begin a farming season without checking the wheels for proper grease.

Plow between the rows.

Ben had a farm implement called a cultivator which was designed to keep weeds and grass out of the field between the rows of planted crops. It was mounted on a frame between two wheels, with two sets of small plows that cultivated the furrows on either side of a row. It was pulled by a team of horses, and the person operating it would either walk or ride, depending on the model. If the operator did not watch the cultivator intently and adjust the angle of the plows when needed, they would wander to one side and plow up the crop.

Likewise, as Ben went through life, he was aware that he was "cultivating" those he was influencing. He was extremely careful not to say or do anything to damage or destroy the person being influenced.

Take the high road.

An excellent example of taking the high road is found in the Bible in 1 Samuel 24:1-7, and in 1 Samuel 26:1-11. On both occasions Saul, the king of Israel, was pursuing David. Saul had three thousand chosen soldiers and was pursuing David with the intent to kill him because of extreme jealousy. Both times, David had an opportunity to kill Saul, but refused to do so, saying, "The Lord forbid that I should stretch out my hand against the Lord's anointed." (1 Samuel 26:11, New American Standard Translation) David understood that God had chosen Saul to be king and had him anointed, and that God would remove him from the throne when the time was right.

Ben knew this principle very well, and did not use revenge to hurt anyone. He would "take the high road" and keep quiet, often when he would like to avenge himself of some wrongdoing by the other person. He was a very honest man, and would not knowingly damage anyone's character.

When the ax gets dull, the best use of your time is to sharpen it.

Ben and his children often chopped wood for their use, and to sell for extra money. They used a double bit ax and kept it extremely sharp. More wood could be chopped with less effort if the ax were kept sharp. When it became a little dull, they stopped chopping wood and sharpened it. That was the best use of their time.

Watch your focal point and don't look back while you are plowing.

When laying out the furrows for a crop, the best way to get straight rows is to fix your eyes on an object on the other side of the field and plow toward that object. If you look back to check on your progress, you will invariably veer off to one side or the other, and your rows will not be straight.

Ben had a son-in-law who plowed with a tractor, and could not resist the temptation to look back to check on his progress. He always had the most crooked rows in the area. Not only were they unsightly, but very hard to cultivate.

When Ben attempted new things in life, he fixed his eyes on his future goal, and never looked back. "Instead of looking back to the past, look forward to the future," he said. "If I look back and lament the past, I damage my chances for success in the future."

Family and friends are more important than money.

Ben was very loyal to his relatives and friends. He considered family his most important asset, and friends his second most important. He would do anything within his power for both. As a result, he was well liked by everyone, and they would do anything for him.

Attend the church of your choice and trust God.

Ben always attended the church of his choice. He didn't get to attend as much as he would have liked. Even so, he and Tildie still trusted God for every aspect of their lives, and they went to church whenever they could. Some may think it is not important to attend church, but Ben disagreed. "Church is where one gets spiritual help and emotional support from friends. Although church attendance and membership will not qualify you as a Christian, it is much easier to live a Christian lifestyle with the help of an extended church family."

FAILING HEALTH

A Riding Cultivator
Ben used a riding cultivator much the same as this one. He
acquired it about 1937, and it was used by him or Loran
for as long as they remained sharecropper farmers.

"I can't sleep," Ben said. "I'm having chest and stomach pains. It feels like indigestion."

"Why don't you get up and take a dose of soda?" Tildie asked.

It seemed to help, so Ben went back to bed. As soon as he lay down, the pain returned. "Try sitting up in the rocking chair," Tildie suggested.

She got up and wrapped a quilt around Ben. He slept the rest of the night in the chair. The next morning, he went about his farm chores. After all, he had corn and cotton to cultivate and he couldn't let a little pain keep him from doing his work.

The summer of 1939 was not being good to Ben. This scenario of having to sleep in a rocking chair to escape the sharp pain repeated itself for the rest of the week, but Ben took it in stride. He was not one to complain and the farm work had to be done. Loran was only eight.

He wasn't big enough to handle the riding cultivator and there was no money for a hired hand.

On Saturday, Roden came by to see if Ben and Tildie needed anything from town. "Your Papa has been having chest and stomach pains all week," Tildie said.

"I'm taking you to a doctor," Roden responded.

"I guess I need to see one. How about Doctor Monroe?" Ben asked.

"I don't like him. Why don't we go to Doctor Lund? He's a really good doctor."

"He would be okay. It doesn't matter to me."

After the examination, the doctor said, "Mr. Parker, you have a stomach ulcer and heart problems. I can give you medication for both, but a change in what you eat will help more than the medicine."

"What changes should I make?"

"You eat salt pork now, don't you?"

"Yes. That and chicken is about all the meat I have."

"You need to cut out salt pork altogether. Wild meat, such as squirrel and rabbit would be best for you. Chicken is second best. Also, don't eat any greasy foods. Stick with baking and broiling, rather than frying. If you eat fried foods, don't fry them in pork lard."

Ben thought a minute. "That's going to be hard to do."

"I know, but if you follow my instructions, you could live in relatively good health for several more years. If you don't, your condition will get worse in a hurry."

Roden dropped Ben off and drove by Francis's house to let him know what the doctor had said. The next Monday, Francis came to visit. "Loran, do you think you could shoot my 22 rifle and hit what you're aiming at?"

"I think I could."

"Let's set up a target and see what you can do."

They went outside and set up a target behind the barn. Francis handed Loran his Remington 22 semi-automatic rifle. "Now, aim at that spot in the center."

After a few shots, Loran was placing the bullet in the center dot almost every time. Francis seemed to be pleased.

"Now, remember this is not a toy. You are only eight years old, but you are old enough to hunt for squirrels and rabbits. Papa needs them instead of salt pork. I want you to keep him supplied with wild game to eat."

"I'll do my best."

"That's all anyone can ask."

It was obvious Francis was concerned about his papa. He would hunt small game himself for Ben to eat, but he couldn't take the time away from his own crops. He was already behind in cultivating his corn and hygear. He also needed to gather some watermelons and take them to town. He needed the money they would bring for a new lister. The old one was worn out.

Loran began hunting squirrels and rabbits, almost every day. Ben was now eating healthier foods. His chest and stomach pains subsided, but he was still weak and couldn't do much work. Loran and Tildie did what he couldn't do.

"Maybe we should raise less hogs and more chickens," Tildie suggested.

"That's a good idea," Ben responded.

Loran took to hunting like a duck does to water. He enjoyed it, and was glad he could do something to help his papa live a better life. Hardly a day went by that he didn't bring home at least one squirrel or rabbit. Sometimes he even brought a quail or two. He was getting fairly good with Francis's rifle.

Later that fall, Loran and his good friend, Albert Eugene Jones, began hunting possums for their skins. Their hides were used to make most of the less expensive fur coats during that era. Albert Eugene and Loran didn't use the rifle for hunting them. It was too dangerous for two young boys to carry a rifle at night. When their dog treed a possum, one of them climbed the tree and brought it back down. They took turns at that chore. When they had enough skins, they took them to town and sold them. They brought 75¢ each, and Loran's part was more than enough to buy everyone a Christmas gift. No longer would the Parker family have to rely on homemade presents. Each of them got a store-bought gift that year, even Ben and Tildie. They hadn't received a Christmas present in many years. They were extremely proud of their young son.

About a month before Christmas, central Oklahoma had an ice storm. It rained slow and steady almost all day, with the temperature well below freezing. As the rain fell, it froze in place. All the trees, grass, weeds and ground in the area were covered with ice. Some tree limbs broke from the sheer weight they were required to bear. Walking was tremendously dangerous. It was almost impossible to stand or walk on the ice.

Ben took an old pair of shoes and drove tacks through the soles, so that they protruded out the bottom about three-eights of an inch. That made a crude, but effective, set of spikes. With them, he could walk on the ice. "I'll do all the chores tonight. I don't want any of you to help. It's too dangerous for you to be walking on this slick stuff."

The ice lasted for two days. During that time, Ben did both the night and morning chores. Between times, Tildie insisted he rest. He was still weak and not used to doing the chores alone.

The next week after the ice storm, Ben came into the house about an hour before sunset. "Loran, where's the rifle Francis left for you to use?"

"Under my bed. I'll get it for you."

"There's a duck on the pond behind the barn. I'm going to try and get it for our supper."

Ben walked to the barn with the rifle. Entering it, he walked softly to the back, stuck the rifle through a large knothole, and fired. He then went to the pond, waded through the thin ice that had formed and picked up a nice, fat mallard duck. His family had roast duck for dinner that night. It was a welcome change from their normal fare.

A few days before Christmas, Ben and Loran cut a small post oak sapling which had already shed its leaves. The small branches were cut off and the ones left were wrapped with green tissue paper. The tree was set up in the living room and decorated with strings of popcorn. That was their Christmas tree, the type most often used by the Parker family. The presents Loran bought were placed under the tree and the family enjoyed a delightful Christmas. Tildie added to the festivities by making a turkey dinner, along with mashed potatoes, gravy and vegetables. After the meal, she served some of her homemade pies and cakes. The family was happy and blessed.

Ben's health seemed a little better that winter, up to February 4, 1940, when his little girl, Lavada, died. The chest and stomach pains returned, and rivaled the pain he felt from losing his young daughter. Tildie and Loran had to do most of the farm chores; Ben's failing health wouldn't allow him to do much work.

In order to help, Artist took a six-month leave of absence from his job at the Convair Aircraft Factory in Fort Worth, Texas. He and Thelma helped Ben plant and harvest his crops that year. Artist and Thelma, along with their two-year old son, James, moved in with Ben and his family. An extra bed was set up in the screened-in porch. They shared that room with Loran. It was a tight fit, but they managed very well. Their second child, a daughter, was born there. They named her Virginia Evelyn.

A FRESH BEGINNING

The Sunday School at the Pikes Peak Schoolhouse
The two children on the lowest step are Loran and Theta. Tildie is
the black-haired lady directly behind them in the very back row. Ben
was not in the picture, as he was on a preaching engagement.

After Ben received the call to return to ministering God's Word, he
immediately set about getting his minister's license reinstated in the
Methodist Church. His first step was to write a letter to the bishop of
the regional Methodist Diocese at Chickasha. In a few days, he got a
reply. The bishop wanted to meet with him, "… to discuss the reasons
for his non-use of the license, and to plan a course of action to get
it reinstated." The bishop suggested a date for the meeting, with the
instructions that if that date wasn't convenient, Ben was to let him know
when he could meet.

Ben replied by return mail, "I'll be there."

On the date of the meeting, Roden took Ben to Chickasha. After
introductions, the bishop said, "According to my records, you had a

minister's license in the Methodist Church from 1907 to 1930. Is that correct?"

"Yes," Ben answered. "I was a layman in the Brock, Texas Methodist Church during that time, until 1929."

"Why did you let your license expire?"

"We moved to Oklahoma. The Depression hit, and I couldn't afford the $2.00 to get it renewed."

"How old are you, Mr. Parker?"

"I'm 53."

"I sense your health is not good. How is your health?"

Ben shifted his position. The meeting wasn't going well. "My doctor has diagnosed me with an ulcer and heart problems, but that shouldn't keep me from preaching."

"Mr. Parker, the fact is you are too old to preach. I'm going to recommend that your license stay inactive, and not be reinstated. I advise you to go home and live out the rest of your days in retirement."

Ben was crushed. He didn't say much on the return trip, and Roden didn't push for a conversation. He could tell his papa was deeply hurt and troubled.

When they got home, Tildie asked, "How did it go?"

"The Bishop told me I'm too old to preach."

"Evidently, God didn't think so. What will you do?"

"I don't know yet."

Ben picked up his Bible and headed for the barn, to the empty stall, to the place where he often spent many hours studying and praying since Lavada's death. He needed some serious private time with his Lord. Nothing else would satisfy him at that time.

"God, I don't understand. I know you called me into the ministry, but the bishop is refusing to give my license back to me."

Ben heard the voice again. "Don't worry, My child. I called you and I will see that you get a license."

Ben breathed a sigh of relief. "Okay, Lord, it's in your hands. I won't worry about it anymore."

The next Monday, Gertrude and Orville came for a visit. "Did you have your meeting with the bishop?" Gertrude asked.

"Yes, but he refused to reinstate my license," Ben answered.

Gertrude was silent for a few seconds. "I have a suggestion. Why don't you join the Church of God and get a license through them. You would have to take a test, but that shouldn't be a problem. You're very knowledgeable about the Bible."

"That's a good suggestion. What are the beliefs of the Church of God?" Ben asked.

"Almost the same as the beliefs of the Methodist Church in their earlier years," Gertrude responded. "About the only difference is we believe in the baptism of the Holy Spirit, but I can show you in the Bible where that is a normal thing for any Christian."

"It's sounding better all the time. Is there a Church of God near here?"

"There's one in Lindsay. Reverend Collins is the pastor. Orville and I will take you there tomorrow, if you like."

Ben was relieved. "I'd be glad to meet with him tomorrow."

"How about if I go with you?" Artist asked. "I'm interested in you getting a license. I think that would be the best thing that could happen to you at this time."

The four of them met with Reverend Collins the next day. After introductions and a short visit, with Ben explaining why they were there, the reverend said, "First, you need to join the church. After that, I will set you forth as a minister, and you will apply for a license. You will need to take a written test based on the Bible. Then, there will be an oral examination by a three-man board consisting of the State Overseer, myself and one other minister."

The next Sunday, Ben and Tildie joined the Church of God in Lindsay. About a month later, Reverend Collins had a special ceremony at the beginning of the service, to set Ben forth for the ministry. As soon as the family got home that day, he wrote a letter to the State Overseer requesting a ministerial examination.

On the day of the assessment, Roden drove Ben to Oklahoma City. He took the written test and passed it with flying colors. Then came the oral part. The State Overseer acted as spokesman for the board.

The Overseer thumbed through Ben's written exam. "Why do you want to get a minister's license?"

"God has called me back into the ministry," Ben replied. "I was a layman in the Methodist Church for 22 years. When the Depression struck, I let my license expire, as I wasn't using it any more."

"Do you see yourself pastoring a church?"

"No. I'm a farmer and have been all my life. I would preach on weekends, with maybe an occasional revival."

"Where would you minister?"

"There are two small country churches and three congregations meeting in school houses within 10 miles of my house. They're too small to support a pastor. They are operated by a board of deacons, and there's only one man who preaches in them. He's a deacon in the Baptist Church at Cox City, and his pastor won't allow him to be gone more than one Sunday a month. Those churches are very much neglected. I would preach in them."

The Overseer's face lit up. "Where do you live?"

"About 10 miles south-west of Lindsay, just north-west of the Pikes Peak School."

"Mr. Parker, I think you are the answer to our prayers. We've been needing a minister in that area. I'm excited that you want to preach there. You'll get your license in about a week."

Ben beamed with delight. "You're an answer to my prayers, too."

As soon as Ben returned from his examination, he wrote a letter to the board of each of the five churches in his area, to set up a schedule for his ministerial work.

Tildie was deep in thought for a few minutes. "Ben, I don't want to just sit at home while you are preaching. Why don't I organize a church in the Pikes Peak School? I'm sure the school trustees would approve it. I could get a few men to act as a deacon board."

"That's a good idea," Ben answered.

When the Oklahoma Territory was organized on May 2, 1890, one of the first things the new legislature did was to divide the rural parts of the territory into square grids of nine square miles. Each grid was designated as a school district, and each district was entitled to a school house. There was no money to do that much building, so each district was responsible for procuring land and erecting the building. After it was completed, each schoolhouse, along with the land it sat on, was dedicated to the Education Department of the Oklahoma Territorial Government. When the Oklahoma Territory and the Indian Territory combined to become a state on November 16, 1907, the new state legislature followed the mandate of the territorial government.

The Pikes Peak School was designated as District #73. It had three trustees who conducted the business of the school and had the honor of hiring teachers, although the Oklahoma Education Department paid the teacher's salaries. Roden was one of the trustees.

When Tildie told Roden what she wanted to do, he set up a trustees' meeting, to be attended by the three trustees, Ben and Tildie, and the teachers, Mr. and Mrs. Pullen. Tildie presented her case for a church to meet in the schoolhouse, including a Sunday school, a morning worship service and a Sunday night service. The trustees agreed, provided that a board of deacons could be formed to oversee the services.

"Mr. Pullen, you're a Christian, aren't you?" Tildie asked.

"Yes, I am."

"I'd like to see you as chairman of the board of deacons."

"I'd be honored to fulfill that position," Mr. Pullen responded. "A deacon board is usually made up of men, but it would be good if Mrs. Parker could be one of the members. This is her idea, and I think she would work harder for fulfillment of this endeavor than any man would."

The trustees agreed, so Tildie became the second member of the deacon board. Later that week, the trustees found another man to be a deacon and services started the following Sunday.

Ben now had six churches within 10 miles of his home. He could preach at each one in turn and complete his rounds in six weeks. That was much better than their situation in the past, when they were lucky to get a licensed minister once each six months.

THE LORD'S WORK

Theta, Loran and Lassie on Loran's bicycle, in front of a wild plum thicket

Near the middle of May, 1940, Ben began ministering again. It was different than when he was a layman in the Methodist Church. Then, he preached occasionally and helped the pastor with visitation. Now, he preached almost every Sunday, in both the morning and evening services. When his farm work would allow it, he preached revivals. They usually lasted one or two weeks.

That summer, Ben was still weak from his illness. Since he walked to his ministry engagements, up to 10 miles each way, he was exhausted when he returned on Sunday nights. He had to rest all day on Mondays. That was no problem. Artist and Thelma did the farm work Ben would normally do. At that time, Thelma's baby girl was less than two months old, but she worked in the fields along with Artist. Tildie cared for the baby while Thelma worked, and also did her share of the farm chores.

"We're glad to do this for Papa," Artist said. "I'm happy he is ministering in the church. I think it's the best thing he could do at this time."

As soon as Ben began ministering, his health started to improve. It was a slow, but steady, process. By the time the harvest was finished, he had most of his strength back. Artist and Thelma could now return to Texas and continue their lives together.

Young Loran, now 10 years old, continued hunting and supplying his papa with wild meat, as the doctor had suggested. The entire family was relieved and pleased that his health was improving.

Ben's message was a simple one: salvation through Jesus Christ and right living as a result of accepting Him as your Savior. The people attending the churches in his area of ministry, although small in number, were extremely happy to have a circuit preacher serving them. At each church, whenever he was scheduled to preach, the members invited their neighbors to the services. Hardly a Sunday went by without someone accepting Jesus as their Savor. Excitement mounted at the churches he served.

The Sunday morning service was almost always evangelistic in nature. Since visitors normally didn't come on Sunday night, Ben usually preached on principles of Christian living in that service. Most of the time, the Sunday night altar call was for believers who wanted to embark on a higher level of right living. When someone was struggling in their walk with Christ, Ben was ready and willing to stay with them all night, if need be, until they felt a release to go home and put into practice what they had learned that evening. He often stayed until midnight working and counseling with someone at the altar. When that happened, he wouldn't get home until 1:00 or 2:00 Monday morning.

Although a quiet man by nature, Ben also had a sense of humor, and often used it to get a point across. Sometimes, upon arriving at a preaching engagement and observing most of the people sitting in the back pews, he would start his sermon by saying, "You can tell the difference between a burlesque show and a church by where the people sit. Since you're sitting in the back, I can see you've come here to have church." He also knew when to quit using humor. He never used that line more than once on the same congregation.

Ben never took an offering for himself. The churches where he preached always took one for him, but it was consistently small. The Depression was not completely over, and people didn't have much money. That was fine with Ben. He made his living by farming and didn't count on the donation for any of his needs. Even if a stipend was not given, he would still preach. That was his calling and he didn't need money to do what his God wanted him to do. Often, he would see something that needed to be done at the church, perhaps a repair that should be made, and would donate his offering to that project.

A few months after Ben began his circuit-preaching ministry, Francis came to visit the family. He had a beautiful young collie in the back of his pickup. Loran walked up to the truck and asked, "Whose dog is that?"

"He's yours," Francis answered.

Loran immediately fell in love with him. "I am going to name him Lassie," he said.

"But Lassie is a girl dog's name," Tildie protested.

"That's okay. I still want to name him Lassie."

Loran had just read the book <u>Lassie</u>, and although the collie was a male, he wanted to name him after the hero in that book. He looked just like the picture of Lassie in the book he had just finished reading. How could he name him anything else?

Lassie was one of the smartest dogs the family had ever seen. He was excellent with livestock, and, at Loran's command, would do anything he wanted him to do. Lassie was eager to help, and he also enjoyed mimicking anything anyone did. At one time, he frightened Evelyn's husband, Raymond, by scratching on the window screen after seeing Tildie scratch on the screen.

The Parker family lived about one hundred yards from a large forest with grazing meadows, and had built a fencerow from their barn to the pasture. It was Loran's job to take the cows to their grazing land after the morning milking and feeding. After getting Lassie, things changed.

He no longer had to take the cows to the pasture. Lassie did that job for him.

Loran would say, "Lassie, take the cows to the pasture."

At that command, he would trot over to the lead cow and say, "Woof," in a low, calm voice. If the lead cow didn't move, he would nip her heel, then drop back on the ground, lying on his belly, and with his head on the ground. In this position, if the cow kicked at him, she would miss. It took only a few times of this procedure for the lead cow to learn that "woof" from Lassie meant, "Go to the pasture."

About four months after getting his new dog, Loran was walking along the road to the south of their house, with Lassie beside him. He observed two men trying to load a cow into a truck. Their neighbor's, the Greggs, had just moved and they could not get one old cow to go into their moving truck. They had left her and sent a truck driver, who made part of his living hauling cattle for other people, to get the cow. The truck driver had brought a helper, but they were not having any luck getting the cow loaded. She would not go up the loading chute, no matter what they did. They tried twisting her tail. They tried whipping her with a whip. They tried pushing her, but nothing worked.

After a few minutes of watching their fruitless effort Loran said, "Mister, would you like me to load that cow for you?"

The truck driver said, "Well, sonny, if you think you can do a better job of loading this cow than I can, go ahead."

Loran turned to his dog and said, "Lassie, put that cow in the truck."

Lassie trotted over behind the cow and nipped her heel, then dropped back, lying on the ground. He knew what the cow would do. She kicked at Lassie, but of course missed. He got up, nipped her heel again and dropped to the ground. The cow kicked at him again. With the third nip on the cow's heel, she very calmly walked up the loading chute into the truck and waited for the men to replace the tailgate.

The truck driver was amazed, and immediately said, "How much do you want for that dog?"

Loran replied, "This dog is not for sale."

About a month after that incident, the Parkers came home from town one day and Lassie was missing. They were sure the truck driver stole him. Francis found out where he lived and drove to his house. He lived about one hundred yards down a slight incline from the road. Francis saw Lassie in the yard, so he parked his pickup at the road and walked down to the man's house.

Francis knocked on the door. When the man came to the door, he asked, "Where did you get that dog?"

"I bought him," the man answered.

Francis retorted, "That is my little brother's dog. I'm going to walk back to my truck and call the dog by his name, and you had better not try to hold him."

Francis went back to his pickup and called, "Lassie, come here."

Lassie came running to him and jumped into the back of his pickup. Francis brought Lassie back to Loran.

About a month later, Lassie was missing again. This time Francis could not find him, so Loran lost his dog. Everyone was sure the truck driver had stolen him again, but hid him somewhere at one of his relatives, where he couldn't be found.

In addition to being a circuit preacher, Ben was also a dedicated farmer and taught his children the value of diligent labor. Even though his lessons were about farming, he was also instilling in them a work ethic that would serve them well in any occupation. All his children were assiduous workers in whatever vocation they entered. They were also astute in managing the funds they earned.

The next spring, Loran brought a booklet to the supper table. It was his job to pick up the mail on the way home from school. The booklet was in the mailbox with the other items. "I can sell White Cloverine salve and get prizes," he said. "If I sell 30 boxes, I can get a 22, single-shot rifle with a 20-inch barrel. That would be shorter than the gun Francis loaned me, and easier for me to handle. I'd like to sell salve and get that rifle."

"What are some of the other prizes?" Ben asked.

"They're mostly toys. I would like to try for the rifle."

"I don't see what it would hurt."

"I think it's a good idea," Tildie said. "Even if you don't sell 30 boxes, you can still get something for your efforts."

Loran filled out the form and ordered 12 boxes. That was all he could get on the first order. If he sold those, he could get 18 on the second one. He sold them in two days, sent the money in and filled out the second form. About a week later, his second order came. He branched out in the neighborhood and sold all of them in a week. Excitedly, he sent the money in, choosing the rifle as his prize. It came in about two weeks. It had a post-style front sight and a "V" back sight.

Loran could hardly wait to try out his new rifle. He set up a target and began sighting it in. Even with the back sight in the lowest notch, the rifle shot an inch high at 20 feet. That would never do. Loran thought a minute. *If I file the "V" down about an eighth of an inch, that will make the back of the rifle come up, thus lowering the impact point of the bullet.* He went to the toolbox and got a triangular file. He carefully filed the "V" the required amount, then filed the top of the back sight the same amount.

About the time he finished, Ben came by. "How are you doing with your new gun?" he asked.

"It shot high," Loran answered. "I think I just took care of that."

"Are you sure you know what you're doing?" Ben asked.

"Yes," Loran said. "I'm getting ready to try it again."

"Carry on," Ben said. "I have some chores to do."

Loran continued sighting in his rifle. With the back sight in the second notch from the bottom, the bullet hit the bull's eye at 20 feet. Perfect.

With a single-shot rifle, one seldom gets a second chance, so Loran began making every shot count. As a result, he quickly became quite good with his new gun. In addition to hunting with it, he also practiced shooting it. He soon got to the point where he could stick a match in the soil 20 feet away and place the bullet in the right position to strike the match as it went by. Small game seldom got away from him, once he drew a bead. He was supplying his papa with even more wild meat than before.

☙

In June of that year, Ben and Loran took employment with a neighboring farmer to chop his cotton. They had already finished that job on Ben's farm. "Ben, I'll pay you $1.00 a day and Loran 75 cents a day," he said.

When Loran found out what they were getting, he said, "Papa, it's not fair. I can chop more cotton than you can and I get paid less than you do."

"I know," Ben answered. "But this farmer won't pay children more than 75 cents a day. We have two choices. We can quit or we can work."

"We need the money, so let's keep working," Loran responded.

It took Ben and Loran three days, working from sunup to sundown, to finish the task. Ben's $3.00 was used to buy some basic supplies; Loran's $2.25 bought a school outfit, with money left over for cartridges for his new rifle.

THE CELLAR

An Underground Cellar
Dirt cellars were used for storing food, as well as shelter from a storm.

Ben knew how to make a cellar. He learned while living in Brock. Although his family did not live in the tornado belt, they were close enough. In the spring and summer months, they went to the cellar often to escape a "Texas Twister."

In addition to storm protection, the underground cellar was also used for storing food. There, the temperature was more constant than in any other structure. It was usually between 50 and 60 degrees at all times. The near-constant temperature helped prolong the shelf life of canned fruits and vegetables. If the crops were scant for a few years, food canned as much as four or more years prior could still be used.

The cellar was also a good place to store root crops such as carrots and potatoes. The temperature was just right and the moist conditions prolonged their usefulness. Almost every cellar, no matter how small, had shelves for canned food and bins for root crops. Also, most of them had benches or wooden boxes for people to sit on while waiting out a storm.

It was the same in Oklahoma. Since tornadoes were common from March to September, almost every sharecropper farm had a cellar. If Ben and Tildie moved to a place without one, he immediately set about constructing it.

Most cellars were produced the same way. After selecting a site that would drain well, a pit was dug about eight feet wide, five feet deep and ten to twelve feet long. A set of dirt steps about three feet wide was dug at one end. A pair of "A" frames was built over the steps and at the other end to hold the ridgepole. It was made from a log about eight to ten inches in diameter. Smaller logs formed the roof, with the large end on the ridgepole and the other on the ground. If available, tarpaper was placed over the log roof to keep dirt from filtering through the cracks. The dirt from the excavation was placed on the logs. Last, a door was assembled to seal the opening over the steps. Some cellars had a six-inch pipe through the roof, with a circular cap on it, for ventilation.

Weeds were not allowed to grow on the dirt roof of a cellar. Their roots collected and held rainwater, funneling it down and allowing the floor to become wet and soggy. Without vegetation, the dirt became compacted and would drain the water off without much of it soaking into the roof.

Most sharecroppers had horror tales about having to go to the cellar during a storm and finding that they were sharing it with snakes or small animals such as rats or opossums. Usually, that experience was the result of carelessness in leaving the door open overnight. Ben and Tildie were careful and didn't have any of those stories to tell.

When Ben and Tildie moved to the farm northwest of the Pikes Peak School in the fall of 1937, it had a cellar, but it was in need of repairs, especially the door. Ben found some used lumber that was still in good shape, made a new door and made the other necessary repairs. It was then ready to receive the food which was to be stored in it.

That cellar received an unexpected use in the spring of 1939. Ben and Tildie's hens had just increased their egg laying, after the long, cold winter doldrums. They provided nice egg boxes in the henhouse, complete with a soft padding of hay, which was changed often. Even so, some of the hens preferred to find other places to lay their eggs. They hid their nests under bushes, in thick weeds, under the house, or any other place they could find. By observing their actions, Tildie could tell the approximate location of their nests. It was then a matter of finding them, so their eggs could be gathered daily.

One old hen was very creative in finding a nesting site. She discovered that Ben and Tildie were leaving the cellar door open during the daytime, to allow it to air out after the damp winter months. She went into the cellar and found some old newspapers. She fashioned her nest in the pile of old papers, and began her daily task of laying eggs.

Tildie discovered where the hen hid her nest by observing her actions. The hen walked toward the cellar door, stopped, and looked around. Then, she walked to the cellar door, stopped, and looked around again. After satisfying herself that no predators were in the area, she popped down into the cellar to lay her egg for that day. In a few minutes, her head was seen sticking up above the base of the door facing. She was standing on the top step, peeking over, looking for predators. She then hopped out of the cellar, and went on her way. The hen repeated this procedure every day, and one of the family members gathered an egg from her nest each evening during the usual egg-gathering time.

There was a rather large, black snake in Oklahoma, which most people called a chicken snake, due to its propensity for dining on eggs and small chicks. This snake would often be five to six feet long and three inches across at the middle of its body. Tildie hated chicken snakes and killed any she saw.

After about two weeks of gathering one egg each day from the cellar hen, her nest suddenly became empty each evening. The third day of finding an empty nest, Tildie announced at supper, "I think a chicken snake is getting the eggs from the nest in the cellar. I watched the hen go down there today, but when I checked her nest, it was empty."

"Do you think the snake is hiding in the cellar?" Ben asked.

"Yes, I do."

"I have to plant our corn field tomorrow. Day after tomorrow, I'll take everything out of the cellar and find him."

Tildie knew the habits of a chicken snake very well. After swallowing an egg, the snake crawls through a tight place to break the egg, to speed up the digestion process. She intended to exploit this habit to catch the snake.

Tildie didn't tell Ben what she planned to do, but she did have a plan. The next morning, she took an egg that was a few days old and placed it in the cellar nest. Then she got a one-gallon glass jug, with a circular glass handle, filled it with water, and placed it beside the nest. She reasoned that the snake was hiding in the cellar, and came out to eat when it smelled a fresh-laid egg. She was giving it a bonanza: two eggs to swallow.

Tildie went about her usual chores, and from her living room window, watched the hen emerge from the cellar. She waited a few minutes, then went down into it. The chicken snake acted just as she thought. It swallowed one egg, then crawled through the jug handle, and swallowed the second egg. Since the handle was too small to allow the eggs to be crushed, it was stuck. It had a large lump on each side of the handle, caused by the eggs it had swallowed.

"Loran, hurry! Bring me a hoe," she called from the cellar.

From the tone of her voice, Loran knew he needed to move fast. He grabbed a hoe and ran for the cellar. Tildie separated the snake's head from its body, and the ordeal was over.

In late August of 1941, the cellar protected the Parker family from the worst tornado they experienced while living in Oklahoma. It was a Saturday, and Ben had gone to a neighbor's house to discuss crop harvesting. The neighbor had agreed to help with Ben's harvest, and in return, Ben would help him. They were deciding when and where to begin.

While he was gone, Tildie noticed a tornado cloud forming to the northwest. It was taking shape in a hurry and was moving toward their house rather fast. Tildie, Loran and Theta stood outside and watched it.

"I hope your papa sees the cloud and comes home before this storm hits," she said. "Just to be on the safe side, I'm opening the cellar door, so we can dash to it when the storm hits."

After Tildie opened the door, she said, "Loran, will you take the lantern down into the cellar and light it?"

"Yes, I will."

He picked up the lantern, retrieved a box of matches and went to the cellar. After lighting the kerosene lantern, he placed it on a wooden box and returned to watch the cloud.

A tornado makes a lot of noise. Anyone who has ever stood by a set of railroad tracks and listened to a steam locomotive pulling 50 loaded freight cars will have some idea of the sound of a tornado. It's loud!

When Tildie heard the tremendous noise and saw the trees about a quarter-mile from their house bending from the strong winds, she said, "It's time!"

The three of them ran to the cellar. Theta went down and sat on a box. Tildie and Loran lingered on the cellar steps, looking for Ben. In a few seconds, they saw him running up the road. He had seen the cloud, almost too late to come home. It would be close. Tildie prayed, "Lord, don't let Ben get caught in this storm."

Ben entered the cellar, closed the door and secured it just as the storm hit. Theta sat on her box, with a worried look. Ben sat on another box, panting from his mad dash to the cellar. Tildie prayed, "Thank you, Lord, for protecting Ben."

Outside, the storm raged in all its fury. The Parker family could hear the ferocity of the tornado. They heard tree limbs being ripped off, the neighbor's wash tub slammed against their house, windows breaking and other sounds of the tornado. They could tell it was a bad one.

When it subsided, they emerged from the cellar. Trash was strewn in a northwest to southeast pattern. A two-by-four, hurled like a javelin by the storm, penetrated the trunk of the small mulberry tree in their front yard. Several corrugated metal panels were ripped off the roof of the barn. Two windows were broken from flying objects. The tornado lifted the roof of the house and twisted it about two feet, leaving it skewed and just sitting on the house. It was no longer attached.

"I can fix the barn," Ben said. "The house is another matter. That will require a carpenter with the right equipment. I'll contact the owner tomorrow about the roof."

Ben found the metal panels from the barn. They were twisted and bent, but he was able to straighten them and re-attach them to the roof. The family picked up the trash and sawed the two-by-four off, leaving it in the tree. It would be near impossible to remove it.

The next day, Ben went to Lindsay to get glass to repair the broken windows and to talk to the owner about repairing the roof.

"I'm not going to repair the roof just yet," the owner said. "I'll let you know in about two weeks what I will do about it."

Near the middle of September, Ben came to the supper table with a dejected look. "I've got bad news again. The owner of this farm isn't going to repair the house. He's bought the land to the south, where the Greggs used to live, and is going to convert both places into a cattle ranch. We have to move again."

"Have you looked for another farm?" Tildie asked.

"Yes and the only one I could find is a mile south of here. It's about the same size as this one, but 20 acres of it is grazing land. The children would have to walk the same distance to school, just from a different direction."

"Go ahead and take it," Tildie responded.

About the middle of November, they moved again.

SMALL BLESSINGS

A Young Billy Goat
Loran and Theta had a good time playing with Billy.

On a spring day in 1942, while at the supper table, Tildie had a worried look. "Ben, we're out of money and almost out of basic grocery items."

"We're also almost out of chicken feed and mash for the hogs. I need to get a job for a few days," Ben replied.

"I have a few eggs to sell, but that won't buy all the things we need. The fryers aren't ready yet."

"I'll go to Lindsay tomorrow and see if I can find a job. I can stay with Francis and Dora, so I won't have to rent a room while I'm there."

The next day, Ben walked to Lindsay and began looking for work. That was nothing new. They had run out of money in the springtime on several occasions, before any crops or livestock were ready to be sold. When that happened, Ben usually went to one of the towns nearby to seek temporary employment.

After a couple of days, Ben found a restaurant owner who needed a cook, and was having a difficult time finding one. He hired Ben for a two-week period while he looked for a permanent one. Ben's wage as a cook was $1.00 an hour, which was more than sufficient for his monetary needs at the time. He was elated to find such a good temporary job.

When the two weeks were over, the owner of the restaurant paid Ben with a check. He went to the First National Bank in Lindsay to cash it. He had his mind on some things he needed to do when he got home, so he was not paying much attention to the teller when she counted out his money. He turned to walk away; then it dawned on him that she had shorted him $10.00. He counted his money and confirmed he was indeed short.

Ben turned to the clerk and said, "You shorted me $10.00."

"I'm sorry," answered the clerk. "It's our policy that we can't correct a mistake after the customer has left the window."

Ben responded, "Okay," and left the bank. He was short more than a day's wages, but he could live with that, so he did not make a scene. That was not his nature.

Ben was honest to a fault, and simply would not cheat anyone, no matter what the circumstances. He also didn't want to be cheated, but he believed that God would help him take care of his needs. If he really needed that $10.00 in the future, his Lord would supply it in some other form. There was no need for him to worry about it.

About two months later, Ben sold some calves at an auction in Lindsay. He went back to the same bank to cash his check. As luck would have it, or providence, the same teller was at the window. When she counted out his money, she made another $10.00 mistake, only on this occasion she gave him too much. Ben was paying attention this time and caught the mistake immediately. He picked up his money and walked away. When he had taken three or four steps, the clerk called out for him to return to the window.

"I gave you too much money," she said.

"The last time I cashed a check here, you shorted me $10.00 and said you could not correct your mistake, because I had left the window," Ben responded.

The clerk turned red, and had a subdued look on her face. She quietly said, "Okay."

Ben had his $10.00 back.

Later that spring, while they were eating supper, Tildie said, "Ben, why don't we get a dozen ducklings? I could raise them to eating size, and that would give us a change in the type of meat we eat."

"That's a good idea," Ben answered. "I'll get them the next time I go to town."

"In the meantime, could you build a pen using small chicken wire?" Tildie asked.

"I'll do it tomorrow," Ben promised.

He built the pen the next day. In one corner, he placed a small duck-house for them to sleep in, and to keep them out of any inclement weather that might come along.

A couple of weeks later, Ben returned from Lindsay with 12 ducklings. He placed them in the pen, and Tildie began feeding them. When they became large enough to find part of their food, Tildie began letting them out during the daytime. A few days later, when she went to the pen to let them out, two of the ducks were dead.

"Ben, did you see the ducks eating anything unusual?" she asked.

"No, I didn't," Ben answered. "I saw them eating grass and some wild seed, but nothing unusual."

The next morning, two more of the ducks were dead. Tildie watched them closely that day. In the afternoon, she observed two of them standing on a red-ant hill, gobbling up the ants as they emerged from underground. When she put them in the pen that afternoon, the two ducks that were eating ants seemed to be sick. The next morning, they were dead. The mystery was solved: red ants were killing them.

"It's a blessing you found what was killing the ducks before the ants eradicated all of them," Ben said.

After the incidents with the ducks, Ben came home one afternoon with a small billy goat, not much more than a kid. One of his neighbors wanted to sell him, and was asking 50 cents for him. Ben bought him.

"He'll be good eating in a few months," Ben said.

Ben and Tildie always warned their children against making pets out of farm animals. They were usually destined to become food for the family or to be sold for needed cash. With the young billy goat, Loran and Theta ignored that rule. His antics were so cute, they couldn't resist. They named him Billy. He followed them everywhere they went, trying to mimic everything they did.

One day in late spring, after school was out, Loran and Theta found two pieces of tin roofing that had blown off the barn.

"Let's make a slide from these pieces of tin," Loran said. "We can use them to slide down the sandstone bank behind the barn."

"That sounds like fun," Theta replied.

Loran folded one end up on each piece of tin, to make crude sleds, and he and Theta used them to slide down the creek bank. On about the third trip, Loran heard a noise and looked up to see the goat sliding down on his behind.

"Watch out!" he called. "Billy is sliding down the bank."

After each trip, Loran, Theta and the goat ran back up the trail and slid down again. After about four times, Loran noticed that the hair on the goat's rump was beginning to wear off.

"We have to do something, or Billy's back end will be sore," he said. "Keep him here, and I'll see what I can find."

Loran went to the barn and found a large piece of cardboard. Returning, he said to the goat, "Billy, sit on this cardboard to slide down."

The goat sat down on the cardboard, and Loran gave him a push. Billy slid down the bank, then ran back up the trail and waited for Loran to position the cardboard again for him. They had a delightful time sliding down their sandstone slide with Billy.

Later, Loran and Theta's pet did become food for the family. Theta refused to eat any of the meat. "That would be too much like eating one of your friends," she said.

NEW GROUND

A Turning Plow
The turning plow was only one of several horse-
drawn farm implements Ben used.

The sharecropper farm Ben found the fall of 1941 turned out to be a
temporary fix. During their one-year stay there, the owner of a larger
and more desirable tenant farm approached him one day while he was
in Lindsay buying supplies.

"Ben, I've been meaning to drive out to see you. I have a proposition
for you."

"Oh! What did you have in mind?" Ben questioned.

"I have a farm one-half mile north of the Pikes Peak School. The
house is in pretty good shape, but the fences are falling down. My
last tenant didn't keep them up. It's a much better place than the one
where you're living now. I'd like you to take it and farm it, rent free, in
exchange for repairing the fences and keeping them, the house and other
buildings in good repair. I'll extend this offer for the rest of your life."

"That sounds like a good deal," Ben responded. "Could I look at it
and give you my answer later?"

"Take all the time you need. You probably won't move until after your crops are harvested anyway. You can let me know later."

Ben looked at the farm and decided it was indeed a desirable arrangement. It was larger, about 80 acres, with 50 acres of farm land. The soil was better than at their present place. Also, the wooded pasture was better. He decided to take it.

Near the end of October, 1942, the gathering of their crops was complete. As soon as the last stalk was harvested, Ben and Tildie began preparing for the move. He wanted to get an early start on repairing the fences. They were in bad shape.

A few days after moving in, Ben contacted the owner. He had a proposal to present. "I've found a 10-acre plot on the back side of the farm which has rich soil and a thick stand of small post oak and blackjack trees," Ben said. "The post oak trees would make good fence posts. I'd like your permission to clear that 10 acres and plant corn there next year."

"You have my permission," the owner responded. "Treat the farm just like you would your own. If there's posts and wood left over, above your requirements, feel free to sell them for the extra money you'll need to feed your family."

Ben and Loran began the long and arduous task of clearing new ground. Loran helped in the evenings after he came home from school, and on Saturdays. Ben did most of the cutting of the smaller trees, along with trimming them and stacking the brush for burning. When Loran helped, they cut down the larger trees, using a two-man crosscut saw. They hauled the logs to the barnyard, where they could be more easily made into posts for the fences, and wood for the heater and cook stove.

It was hard work, but they were used to it. Even though Loran was only 12, he was already a good worker. Ben was strong for his size, and Loran's muscles hadn't fully developed, so they devised a method of loading the logs into the wagon. For smaller logs, Ben picked up the larger end and Loran the smaller. For bigger ones, they both lifted the larger end onto the front wagon wheel. Loran then balanced it while Ben lifted the smaller end into the wagon.

The two of them also devised a method for splitting the big logs into fence posts. Ben had splitting wedges and a sledgehammer, but that method was too slow. They used their double-bit axes to do the job in less time. Ben would sink his ax into the end of a log. Loran would straddle the log, and sink his ax into the crack produced by Ben's ax, about six inches from his. That would loosen Ben's ax. He would then sink his in the ever-increasing crack about an inch from Loran's. This procedure was repeated until the log was split. They could divide a large log into two pieces in about a minute, much less time than would be required by using splitting wedges.

The 10-acre new ground they cleared produced a bumper crop of corn the next year. They gathered six large wagonloads from it. Other 10-acre plots in the area produced only about three wagonloads.

While they were gathering corn that fall, an amusing event occurred: A grasshopper flew up Ben's trousers. He suddenly began dancing up and down, shaking his pants leg. After several hops, he jerked his trousers off. Loran had a good laugh at his dad's comical antics. At the time, it wasn't funny to Ben. The grasshopper was scratching his leg, and he needed to get it out in a hurry.

As Ben put his pants back on, he laughed. "I guess I did present a funny sight, dancing around and jerking my pants off."

The summer of 1943 arrived, and with it, another new ground, this time for Loran. Ben decided it was time for him to learn how to cut broomcorn. It was the best-paying farm related, summertime job in the area. It also had a longer harvest season than other summer crops. By teaching Loran this job, he set a precedent that served his family well for several years.

Ben had a neighbor, Fred Baker, who was a broomcorn harvest contractor and field boss. He would find fields that were ready for harvest, contract the job and hire the people to get the job done. Ben and Loran hired on to be part of his crew. He lived about a quarter-mile from the Parkers, and drove by their house on the way to Lindsay every morning during broomcorn season. Ben and Loran rode to town with him in his flatbed truck. He picked up the rest of his crew there, then drove to the field being harvested that day.

After they had been working for Mr. Baker for a couple of weeks, he took his crew to the field of Harry Moore. Mr. Moore was well known throughout the area for being a tight-wad. He simply would not buy anything unless he was getting a fantastic deal. At Mr. Moore's field, the crew got off the truck and began preparing to go to work. Mr. Moore looked the crew over, then said to Mr. Baker, "I'll take every hand you have except that kid there," pointing to Loran.

"You'll take that kid too, or the whole crew goes back to town," Mr. Baker retorted.

What Mr. Moore didn't know was that Loran was very fast with his hands and could cut more broomcorn than anyone else in the crew. Loran cut the broomcorn from his row and about a third of Ben's row, and the two of them would be ahead of anyone else in the field.

Mr. Moore watched Ben and Loran all morning. Ben noticed it first. "I wonder why Mr. Moore is watching us."

"I don't know," Loran responded. "We haven't done anything to make him suspicious. As long as we do our job, he has no reason to watch us."

By noon, Mr. Moore satisfied himself that the kid he was trying to fire was the best worker in his field. He never questioned Mr. Baker's judgment again.

Ben and Loran didn't know about the conversation between the owner and the field boss at the time. Mr. Baker related the conversation to Ben later.

Most people in Mr. Baker's crew didn't take their lunch to work. There was no way to preserve it in the hot, humid weather prevalent in Oklahoma in the summertime. It would spoil before noon. Instead, Mr. Baker brought his crew to the nearest town for them to buy dinner.

Broomcorn cutting wages that first year were 75 cents an hour and they could buy a dinner for about 50 cents. After eating, Ben and Loran usually bought an ice cream cone for dessert. It cost only five cents, and they were used to having something sweet after every meal. The first few times they ate ice cream after a meal, most of the other workers told them they would "burn out" that afternoon. There was an old wives tale saying that eating ice cream before working in the sun would cause heat prostration, or some such thing. When they didn't burn out after several times of eating ice cream at noon, the rest of the crew decided it was safe, and began getting a cone for themselves after their dinner.

In the spring of 1944, Ben's family broke new ground again. A natural gas company was laying a pipeline from a gas well in Cox City to Lindsay, for the purpose of supplying the residents there with gas for heating and cooking. The shortest route came across the middle of Ben's cotton field. The representative from the gas company had already made a deal with the owner of the farm to cross his land. He then came to Ben's house to negotiate a contract for the cotton they would destroy while laying the pipeline.

"We'll pay you what you would make on your cotton crop this year," the representative said. "Just estimate how much you would harvest, and we'll pay you the average price for it. We won't destroy all your cotton. You can harvest the rest of it and sell it. That will be a bonus for you."

"That's more than fair," Ben responded.

"Also, we need a right of way across your field, to make any repairs on the pipeline that might be required in the future. For that inconvenience, we will furnish gas for your heating and cooking needs, at no cost to you, for the rest of the time you stay at this place. You will need to buy the stoves and dig the trench from the pipeline to your house. We'll lay the pipe and do the hookups to your appliances."

"That can be arranged," Ben responded.

Ben took part of the money the company paid for his cotton crop and bought a gas cookstove and a heater. Loran dug the trench. About a month later, the company connected the gas to their new appliances. Tildie was ecstatic as she began cooking on her new stove. No longer would she have to build fires for cooking. After preparing meals on a wood-burning stove for 39 years, her new range and oven was a heavenly blessing. She could control the heat better. She no longer had to rely on intuition when heating her oven. To test the heat on her wood-burning oven, she opened the door and "felt" the heat with her hand. Her new one controlled the heat at the correct temperature for whatever she was baking.

No longer would Ben have to chop wood for their domestic needs. No longer would he have to get up early to build a fire to heat the house. All he had to do now was turn a lever and light a match.

During the summer of 1944, Francis came for a visit. "Now that you don't have to cut wood, and have more time, I have a suggestion for you. I've found a cream separator and an icebox. Why don't you buy another milk cow or two and begin selling cream to the produce house in Lindsay? You'll need to keep the cream in the icebox during the week, then take it to town on Saturday. You could use the extra skimmed milk to feed out a few hogs for sale. The only cost after buying the cows and hogs would be 50 pounds of ice a week, and it would bring in a steady income for you."

Ben was in silent prayer for a few seconds. "That sounds like a good idea. I'll talk it over with Tildie and let you know."

Ben and Tildie decided to accept Francis's offer. He delivered the cream separator and icebox. Ben and Tildie bought two more milk cows and four shoats, and they were in a new business.

Although the income was small, the weekly sale of cream brought in a steady paycheck. It was a great help in alleviating their money worries. Ben and Tildie thanked God for His provisions and blessings.

THE BAPTIZING

A Baptizing
Farm ponds were used for baptizing during the Great Depression.

During Ben's tenure as a circuit preacher, revival meetings were a common occurrence in Oklahoma churches, both large and small. Ben usually held two or three a year. A typical one for Ben was eight days: from Sunday to Sunday. Also, a few other ministers in the area held revival meetings.

In addition, street preaching was a common sight. A minister would set up on a street corner, often standing on a wooden soap box, and begin preaching; thus the saying, "get on your soap box." People gathered around the minister and listened to his sermon.

During those days, the town of Lindsay, Oklahoma was often treated to the sermons of a black street preacher. Lindsay was at the end of the railroad line. At 3:00 each afternoon, a tiny train called the Dinky arrived from Pauls Valley. It consisted of an engine, one car and a caboose. It stayed for two hours, then returned. The black preacher often arrived on the Dinky, ministered on a street corner until almost 5:00, then caught the train back to Pauls Valley. He was always careful to be on time for the return trip. Lindsay had an ordinance prohibiting black people from being in their city limits after dark.

Near the end of September, 1944, Tildie decided it was time for a revival at the church in the Pikes Peak Schoolhouse. "Ben, will you be busy next week?" she asked.

"Why do you ask?" Ben questioned.

"We need a revival at the Pikes Peak Church."

"I'll be busy," Ben answered. "Our corn will be ready for harvesting. Since Loran is in school, I'll have to gather it myself. I can attend the revival, but I wouldn't have time to study for sermons."

"Then, who should I get?" Tildie questioned.

"You could get the Deacon."

"He would be okay. I'll contact him."

The Deacon was a preacher who served on the church board at the Cox City Baptist Church. Most people didn't know his name. They just called him Deacon.

The Deacon agreed to hold an eight-day revival beginning the first Sunday in October.

Each day that week, Ben quit gathering corn in time to get ready for church. Ben, Tildie, Loran and Theta attended services each night.

On Wednesday night, when the altar call was given, Loran went down and accepted Jesus as his savior. Ben and Tildie were ecstatic.

By Saturday, several people had made the decision to follow Jesus, so the Deacon arranged for a baptismal service to be held at 3:00 on Sunday afternoon. It was held at a small farm pond about three miles northeast of Pikes Peak.

After dinner that Sunday, the Parker family got in their wagon and went to the baptism. Loran would be baptized and they didn't want to miss his important event.

On the way to the service Ben said, "Loran, I hope you realize that baptism doesn't save you. Trusting in Jesus is what saves you."

"I know," Loran answered. "I've been studying the Bible. I understand that baptism is merely an outward sign of an inward condition: a statement to the world that you have accepted Jesus Christ as your savior."

When the Parker family arrived, the Deacon asked, "Ben, would you like to baptize your son? I know the evangelist usually baptizes his converts, but I'm sure it would mean a lot to both of you for you to baptize him."

"I'd be delighted," Ben answered.

Loran was baptized by his father that day.

HOG KILLING TIME

Dipping Vat, made from a 50-gallon drum.

A Three-Legged Cast Iron Kettle, used to cook lye soap or render lard.

Before the introduction of packaged meats in super markets, rural folk butchered their own. One event, usually a community affair, was hog killing time. Neighbors used the barter system for many of their requirements. Hog killing was one of those needs.

Hog killing time always started the next day after the first hard freeze in autumn, usually about November 15. Cold weather was needed to keep the meat from spoiling before the curing salt had time to do its job. As long as there was a hard freeze every night, hog killing continued until all neighbors had their supply of meat in the smokehouse. If the weather warmed slightly, it was postponed until the next hard freeze.

Hog killing time not only allowed the community to help each other; it was also a social event. Rural people often used this occasion to catch up on the local news. They worked together, talked, shared meals and, in general, had a good time. It brought them together on a much higher social level than the circumstances suggested.

Hog killing was done in a much different manner than butchering other animals, such as beef. Before the event, a dipping vat was constructed. Most people used a 50-gallon steel barrel for that purpose. The base of the barrel was usually placed on the ground. A "V" shaped stand was constructed at the right height to allow the barrel to be at a 30-degree angle when the lip was placed in the "V". This stand was usually made of concrete blocks and mortar, or welded steel. After the vat was in place, a trench was dug under it, to make a fire pit.

Early on the morning of the event, enough water was poured into the vat to bring it to about two-thirds of the way to the lip. Then a fire was kindled under it, usually with dried oak wood. While the water was heating, other preparations were done.

When the water began boiling, it was time to kill the first hog. The killing was usually done using a 22-caliber rifle. The hog was then stuck at the base of the neck, with a long, sharp knife. Most of the blood was allowed to drain out before it was taken to the dipping vat.

The dipping job required from two to four men, depending on the size of the hog. The men doing the dunking put on heavy leather gloves, then picked the hog up and placed him in the boiling water, on his belly and head first. The purpose of dipping was to cause the hair to turn loose at the roots. If he was dipped properly, scraping with a dull knife removed all the hair from his body, including the roots. After about a minute, he was removed from the vat and tested to see if the hair could be scraped off. If so, he was turned over on his back and dipped again. Then he was reversed and dipped butt first, two more times.

After the dipping, a slit was made on his back legs, to expose the large tendons found there. Using a special-made single tree with a hook on each end, these tendons were hooked, and the hog was hoisted, by a block and tackle or by manpower, so he hung with his heels at about level with the top of an average man's head. The hair was scraped off, and the butchering process begun. As each part was removed: shoulder, tenderloin, bacon slab, ham, etc., it was rubbed liberally with curing salt and hung in the smokehouse.

As a general rule, country folk usually butchered about one 300-pound hog for each two people in the family. A 450-pound hog would feed three people. Since most couples in those times had large families, they usually killed three or more hogs each fall.

When the butchering was done, the work was far from being over. There was sausage to make, hog lard to render, lye soap to be cooked and hogs-head cheese, for those families who liked it.

Sausage was made from parts not usually cooked as a meat dish. The meat was removed from the bone and ground. Then, it was mixed with spices, such as sage and chili powder, and placed in a sausage bag made from cleaned and sterilized intestines from the hog.

Clean, white fat with no impurities was used to make lard for frying and cooking. Most rural people had a large, three-legged cast iron kettle which was used for rendering lard. The legs of the pot were placed on bricks, concrete blocks or rocks, and a fire built around its base. The fat from the hog was placed in the pot. When the fat began melting, the person making the lard began stirring. It was stirred constantly until completely melted. It was then poured into containers, such as half-gallon jars, and sealed.

Fat which was yellowish in color, or with small impurities, was used to make lye soap. Before canned lye was available, it was made using alkali water, by the following method: A "V" trough was constructed, leaving the bottom a little loose. The trough was filled about two-thirds full of wood ashes from a fireplace or stove. Water was poured into the trough to completely fill it. The water was allowed to leach through the ashes, and the drippings were caught. That procedure was repeated until enough alkali water was made for the amount of soap needed.

Equal amounts of alkali water and animal fat were placed in a large pot, often the same one used to render lard. Fat from other animals could be used, such as raccoons, opossums, bears, etc. The mixture of alkali water and fat was then heated. As soon as the fat began melting, the one making lye soap began stirring, and stirred constantly from then on to the end of the process. The mixture was brought to a boil, then the heat was reduced to medium. The mixture was boiled, using medium heat, until the water had evaporated. When the mixture stopped bubbling, the water had evaporated, and the soap making was done. The liquid soap was then poured into a flat pan and allowed to cool. When the mixture set, it was cut into squares.

Lye soap was a necessity in those days. It was the only laundry product which would remove the reddish color from clothes which had come in contact with the clay soil prevalent in Oklahoma. One could also kill unwanted insects, such as chiggers, by taking a bath with lye soap.

Ben's family didn't like hogs-head cheese. They removed the brains, which were used to make a breakfast food which rural folks considered a delicacy—scrambled eggs and brains. The head was then boiled, and the meat scraped off to be used as dog food.

In November of 1943, Ben's neighbor, Houston McKenzie, dropped in for a short visit. "It looks like we're going to have a hard freeze tonight," he said. "If so, would you be willing to help me with my hog killing tomorrow?"

"Sure," Ben answered. "Would it be all right for me to bring Loran? Between the two of us, we can make you a good hand."

"Yes, bring him."

"Okay. What time do you want us?"

"About 8:00 would be fine."

"We'll be there."

Ben hadn't eaten any salt pork since his doctor suggested he should stop eating it. He was butchering only one hog per year, to tide the family over during the spring months when squirrels and rabbits were raising their young and the chickens weren't yet fryers. Loran didn't hunt during that time, and his family needed the meat. Even though his neighbors couldn't fully reciprocate at his hog-killing time, Ben always helped them with theirs.

Ben and Loran arrived the next morning on schedule. Loran leaned his rifle against a mulberry tree, and they joined the others at the dipping vat. Mr. McKenzie had built the fire earlier, but the water hadn't yet reached the boiling point. The men were standing around the fire, talking about the weather and reminiscing about old times. After about 30 minutes, the water began boiling. Time to kill the first hog.

"Now comes the part I hate," Mr. McKenzie said. "My first shot almost always addles the hog, and I have to shoot him two or three times. He stands there squealing, and he excites the other hogs so much that it is more difficult to kill them."

"Why don't you let Loran shoot him?" Ben suggested. "He kills all of ours, and he's never had one to squeal."

Mr. McKenzie thought a minute. He had heard rumors about Loran's abilities with a rifle. Here was a 13-year-old lad who was reputed to be able to strike a match with a 22 rifle, and shoot an opossum's eye out at night by holding a flashlight alongside the barrel. Maybe he would be the one to shoot the hogs.

"I'd gladly turn that job over to someone else. Loran, would you be willing to shoot him?"

"I sure would."

"Would you like to use my rifle?"

"No, I'm not familiar with it. I know my rifle, and know how it shoots."

Loran retrieved his rifle. Mr. McKenzie looked at it. "Do you think that pea-shooter will do the job?"

"It'll do the job."

The men walked to the hog pen. It was the same as most others in the area, constructed with four-inch hog wire.

"Loran, what do you want me to do?" Mr. McKenzie questioned.

"How many hogs will you be killing?"

"Three."

"Move the feeding trough over by the fence. Mix the amount of feed you usually give them and pour about one-third of it into the trough."

Mr. McKenzie complied. "Which one do you want first?" Loran asked.

"The one with the white stripe over his shoulder."

Loran would have to be extremely accurate. There is a spot in the front of a hog's head, about the size of a quarter, where the skull is thin enough for a 22 bullet to penetrate into the brain. Miss that spot, and you have a squealing hog on your hands. He won't be able to run. He will just stand there and squeal. If you are forced to stick him before he's dead, he will squeal even louder. That's the origin of the saying "squeal like a stuck pig".

Loran walked around the pen to the feeding trough. Selecting a 22 short cartridge, he placed it into the chamber of his gun and squatted in front of the selected hog. Making sure the bullet wouldn't strike the fence wire, he traced an imaginary line from the base of the left ear to the right eye, and from the right ear to the left eye. Drawing a bead on the spot where the lines intersected, he gently squeezed the trigger. When the rifle discharged, the hog's legs collapsed and he dropped to his belly, without making a sound. Two of the men caught his back legs and dragged him away from the feeding trough. The other hogs continued eating as if nothing had happened.

The men began preparing him for the dipping vat. Mr. McKenzie looked at Loran. "Where were you during all my other hog-killing times?"

Loran smiled and answered, "Growing up."

FOOTPRINTS

Footprints in the Sand
Ben left footprints in the sands of south-central Oklahoma.

Ralph Waldo Emerson once said, "Go not where the path may lead. Go instead where there is no path and leave a trail."

Not everyone has the good fortune, or luxury, or inclination, or desire, or necessity to go where there is no path. Most of us travel where others have often trod. That doesn't mean we are destined to lead a boring, uneventful, unfulfilled life. As we traverse a well-traveled path, we can leave our own unique footprints in the sands of time: our own well defined trail for others to follow.

Paul of old—the author of most of the New Testament—knew the value of following auspicious footprints when he wrote, "Follow me as I follow Christ." The direction he took along the path of life was worthy to be imitated, and would bring the disciple to a fulfilling and worthwhile conclusion.

Ben knew the value of emulating a disciple of Christ. Although he did not intentionally set out to leave a trail for others to follow, he left one nonetheless. He was merely doing what his Lord wanted him to do, but the footprints he left, if followed, would bring contentment, peace and fulfillment.

Ben was honest to a fault. He believed in, and practiced, the concept of an honest day's work for an honest day's pay, an honest measure for an honest cost, and do unto others as you would have them do unto you.

Ben was faithful to his spouse, his family and his friends. Although some may find excitement and adventure in being unfaithful to their mate, that was not his style. If he acted a certain way while around his family and acquaintances, you could be certain he would act the same way in any situation.

Ben was a diligent worker, whether laboring for himself or another. No task was too menial if it contributed toward his goal of keeping the family fed, clothed, sheltered and happy.

Ben possessed the virtue of commitment. He was loyal to all: spouse, family, friends and God. He would do nothing to bring disgrace on anyone; and especially to his Lord. Each needed task was done with undaunting tenacity.

Ben had unusual faith, not only in God, but also in those with whom he came in contact, and in himself. To him, a man's word was as binding as any contract. If he said he would do something, you could count on it being done.

Anyone would do well to follow Ben's footprints as he traveled the trails of life. The world would be a better place if everyone followed his example.

A good tracker can tell volumes about the animal whose tracks he is following. He can tell you which animal made the tracks. Often he can tell whether the animal is male or female. He can tell whether the animal is in a hurry or is taking a leisurely stroll. He can tell if the animal is feeding along the way, or is going somewhere.

Human footprints are no different. Ben left literal footprints in the sand and dust along the dirt roads of south-central Oklahoma. Many of his neighbors and family knew his footprints, and usually knew when he passed their house going to a preaching engagement.

When he began his circuit-preaching ministry, Ben's family mailbox was part of a group of mailboxes on the main road from Lindsay, Oklahoma, two miles from their house. One day, not long after Ben began ministering, Tildie went to the mailbox. Their neighbor who lived a quarter-mile north of the mailboxes arrived at the same time.

"Ben must have preached at the church in the See Chapel School last Sunday," he commented.

"Yes, he did," Tildie answered. "How did you know?"

"I saw his tracks in the sand near our house yesterday. They went both ways. See Chapel is the only church that direction."

And so it went. Often family members or neighbors would remark, "Ben must have preached at such and such a place. I saw his footprints."

One Monday afternoon in the spring of 1946, Roden came by on his way to town. After visiting for a time, he asked, "Mama, are Papa's Sunday shoes worn out?"

"I don't know," Tildie answered. "I can check."

She went to the closet and returned with Ben's good shoes. Turning them over, she saw a hole in the sole of each shoe, where the ball of the foot rests.

Roden explained, "I saw his footprints in the sand near my house this morning. They showed a hole in each shoe."

Ben had walked more than 10 miles to a preaching engagement that Sunday, in worn out shoes. He knew money was scarce, and figured he could wear them a couple of more times before being forced to buy a new pair.

A few minutes later, Ben came in from doing some farm chores. "Come with me to town," Roden said.

He took Ben to Lindsay, to the Williamson Dry Goods Store, and bought him a new pair of dress shoes. He couldn't bear seeing his papa walking to a ministering appointment in worn out shoes.

A SPECIAL TREE

A Hackberry Tree

Every sharecropper farm occupied by Ben and his family had trees of some type. Most of them had peach orchards, with the Elberta being the most abundant variety. That was a blessing for the family, since the Elberta was an excellent peach, both for eating and canning. The orchard was almost always on the north side of a hill, to keep the trees cool for a longer period in the spring. This would encourage them to bloom later, reducing the risk of frost damage to the young fruit.

Many other types of trees could be found on most sharecropper farms. Willows and cottonwoods were prevalent near ponds and streams. Oaks, primarily blackjack and post oak, grew in abundance in the soils of the drier hillsides. One sharecropper farm they occupied had a small, wild plum thicket to the east of their front yard. Although miniature in size compared to the domestic variety, the wild plums made excellent jams, jellies and desserts.

Various trees were desirable for many and diverse reasons. Oaks supplied excellent firewood: green oak for the heater and seasoned oak for cooking. It burned slowly, and with an extremely hot flame. Peaches and plums supplied fruit to help feed the family. Their small limbs were also often used as switches, to persuade the children in the family to be on their best behavior. Cottonwoods made reasonably good firewood, but were better suited to reducing soil erosion. Willows also helped to keep the soil from being washed away, as well as being a fair emergency food for livestock, in case of a famine.

When Ben and his family moved to the farm one-half mile north of the Pikes Peak school, in November of 1942, they observed a rather large tree in the yard. It stood tall and majestic against the gray sky of early winter. Its leaves had already dropped, and the bare limbs displayed a pleasing pattern of forms and shapes. Theta was drawn to it from the beginning.

"That should make a nice shade tree for next summer," she remarked.

"It sure should," Ben answered.

The tree was fascinating to Theta. She had never seen one larger than an Elberta peach on the other farms where they lived. She kept going outside to gaze at her special tree.

"How tall do you think it is?" she asked.

"Oh, I'd say almost 50 feet," Loran answered.

"It's also wide. How wide would you say it is?"

"Maybe 35 or 40 feet," Ben said.

"What kind of tree is it?"

"I don't know," Ben responded. "Loran, do you know?"

"I don't know, either," Loran replied. "When it puts out leaves next spring, we should be able to tell what kind it is."

All winter Theta kept a watch over her tree. She became familiar with every inch of the trunk by feeling the bark and studying its patterns. She gazed into its branches and memorized the shape of each one. She was enthralled, not only by its size, but by its shapely beauty. She observed her tree often that winter. The smokehouse was on the northwest side of the tree and the henhouse on the northeast side, so it would supply shade for both during the hot summer months. Every time she had to go to the henhouse to gather eggs, or to the smokehouse, she had to pass under her tree.

Early the next spring, Theta came into the house in a run. "My tree has leaves on it," she exclaimed.

Ben and Loran went outside. The tree had budded and was loaded with clusters of tiny greenish, elliptical flowers.

"Do you know what kind of tree it is?" Theta asked.

"Not yet," Ben said. "I'm not familiar with its leaves or flowers."

"Wait a few weeks," Loran replied. "Maybe then we can tell what kind it is."

A few weeks later, the leaves were full size, and tiny, cherry-like fruit had developed.

"It's a hackberry tree," Ben announced.

"Is the fruit good to eat?" Theta asked.

"Yes, but there's not much to it," Ben answered. "It's mostly seed."

Later that summer, Theta came outside and observed Loran sitting in her special tree, eating hackberries. There isn't much to eat in a hackberry. The small, quarter-inch fruit is almost all seed. It has a very thin layer of fruit between the seed and the skin. One has to eat a number of them to garner much nourishment.

"Would you bring me some hackberries?" she pleaded.

"Sure."

Loran picked some berries and climbed down.

"Here are a few. That's all I could carry while climbing down the tree. Eat them, then I'll teach you how to climb the tree to get your own."

"I've never climbed a tree this big before."

"It's easy, and it's also fun."

Theta ate the berries Loran brought, then looked longingly into the tree. She was a little frightened at the thought of climbing it. The tree looked foreboding to a nine-year old who had never climbed one that large before.

"You're too short to reach the first limb," Loran said. "I'll get a ladder for you." At almost 13 years, he was rather tall and didn't need one.

Theta climbed the ladder.

"There's a limb about even with your head," Loran instructed. "Take hold of it with both hands. Now, place your foot on the limb just above the ladder. Pull yourself up until you are standing on that limb."

Loran climbed just below Theta, ready to catch her if she fell. When they reached an appropriate height, Loran said, "Sit on this limb with your feet on the one below it. That way, you can keep your balance. There are lots of hackberries all around you. Pick them and enjoy."

Theta savored the fruit of her special tree. As she sat on that limb eating the hackberries within her reach, she began to look around. The world looked different from that height, and she had a unique feeling of accomplishment.

"This must be the biggest tree in the world," she remarked.

"Oh, no," Loran responded. "Come with me to the creek, and I'll show you elm trees that are much bigger."

"That's okay. This one is big enough for me."

Before they finished their snack, Ben walked under the tree, going to the smokehouse. Theta dropped a seed, and it tapped Ben's shoulder on the way to the ground. Looking up into the tree, Ben questioned, "What are you two doing up there?"

"Eating hackberries," Theta responded.

"Be careful," Ben admonished. "We don't want any broken bones from a fall."

"We're being careful," Loran replied.

"Loran, when you're through there, would you come to the barn?" Ben asked. "I have something I want you to do."

"Sure," Loran answered. "We'll be through here in a minute. I'll be there shortly."

As Ben made his way to the barn, Loran said, "I need to help Papa. Can you climb down by yourself?"

"I'd rather you stay to help me, if I need it," Theta answered.

They descended from the tree and Loran headed to where his papa was.

Loran and Theta climbed that tree many times over the next six years. Its fruit, although scant, made a good between-meal snack. In its branches, Theta felt secure and contented. In its shade, she was cool and comfortable. It was her special spot.

After all these many years, that old hackberry tree is gone. It seems sad, in a way, but even special trees don't last forever. Just like people, they cease to exist, and others arrive to take their place. Now, in its stead stands one of its offspring. Its replacement is a much smaller tree and will probably never grow to the size of its parent. The tree Loran and Theta knew had the advantage of being in an area where chickens were grown. Their droppings provided fertilizer and changing their water troughs gave the tree extra moisture. The new hackberry will rely only on the rains nature brings for its nourishment. Standing on the crest of a hill, and lacking the ready-made fertilizer and moisture from a chicken pen, it will never become as majestic as the one it replaced.

The spot is bare, the tree is gone,
But not forgotten, for it lives on
In the mind of one who, as a child,
Climbed for its fruit, so sweet and mild.

May I live life while here below,
Just as that tree, so men will know,
     For weary travelers I did my part,
And bore the fruit of a servant's heart.
     (L H P)

CHANGING PLACES

A Horse-Drawn Planter
This planter is much like the one Ben used.

In early December, 1943, Tildie met Loran and Theta as they came up the road from school. "Loran, your papa isn't doing well," she said. "It's getting harder for him to keep up with the farm chores. He's used to doing everything, and his pride keeps him from asking you to do more of the work."

"Don't worry, Mama. I'll start doing more and won't mention it to him."

"When the crops need planting next spring, do you think you could run the lister? That's getting very difficult for him."

"Sure, I can operate it. I'm 13 and I've done about everything there is to do on a farm. I can handle it."

Tildie looked a little worried. "I hate to put this on you at such a young age. You're only a seventh-grader."

"Don't worry. I can handle it. It's time for me to start growing up a little anyway."

"I sure appreciate your willingness to take on such a heavy load. Your papa does, too, but it's difficult for him to admit that he can't handle it any more."

Loran was deep in thought for a time. "What about Papa's preaching? Will he continue that?"

"Yes, he would like to continue serving the churches in the area. That's important to him."

Loran smiled. "I'm glad. I'll take on even more of the chores on the weekend."

"I'll help you all I can," Tildie responded.

"I can help with the cooking and house cleaning," nine-year-old Theta said.

"Thank you," Tildie answered. "I appreciate that."

Roles reversed that day. Loran began doing the major part of the farming operation. Tildie did more of the chores. Theta did more cooking and housework. Ben did the lighter work, but continued making the farming decisions. The agribusiness operation went smoothly, and the four of them worked as a close-knit family to keep crop-raising, the main source of their livelihood, on an even keel.

Ben continued preaching on the weekends. Each Saturday afternoon, Tildie insisted he take a nap to rest for his Sunday walk to his ministry engagement. At first, Ben didn't want to, but, as time marched on, he realized he needed that Saturday rest. Also, on Mondays, Ben was exhausted from his strenuous Sunday schedule, and needed to rest almost all day. Loran, Tildie and Theta did all the work on those days.

Ben and Tildie had a flock of 15 brown leghorn hens. They were good egg layers, and they could almost count on 15 eggs a day from their flock. Even though they didn't bring in much money, selling the eggs to the Lindsay produce house was an important part of their income. They usually sold six or seven dozen eggs each Saturday. That helped buy the necessities they couldn't grow.

In February, 1944, Francis acquired a brown leghorn rooster, which he brought to Ben and Tildie. "You can get almost twice the price for fertile, purebred eggs than what you are getting for eating eggs," he said. "Why don't you turn this rooster loose with your hens? Their eggs will be fertile in about two weeks."

"That's a good idea," Ben answered. "We'll do it."

It turned out that the rooster was extremely territorial. Anyone coming close to his domain was subject to being flogged. He was cautious about attacking adults, but children were another matter. Any child who didn't run when he strutted toward them would be flogged. His spurs were short and dull, but he could bruise them with his wings. Family and friends with young children knew to keep them away from his territory.

Theta was small for her age, and looked like a child to the rooster. She was often the brunt of his aggressive behavior. That presented a problem, as she often gathered the eggs for Tildie at the end of the day. If the rooster was near the henhouse, she got chased back into the house.

One day, about sunset, Tildie asked, "Theta, could you gather the eggs for me? I'm busy now with other things."

"Sure," she answered.

She picked up the basket and left for the henhouse. About two minutes later, she came running back into the house.

"Did the rooster chase you?" Ben asked.

"Yes," she answered. "He was guarding the henhouse, and he came strutting toward me. I ran."

"Don't worry about it. I'll gather the eggs in a few minutes," Tildie said.

"Why don't we just get rid of that rooster?" Theta asked.

"We need that rooster," Loran answered. "He helps us make money. You'll just have to live with him."

"Okay, but keep him away from me."

Loran always carried a slingshot in his back pocket when he was doing chores or plowing the fields. Rabbits were plentiful, and he often got one for supper while performing his duties on the farm. A rifle was awkward to carry, so he used his trusty slingshot.

One day, as Loran was feeding the livestock, the rooster slipped up behind him and flogged his legs. As Loran turned, he instinctively pulled the slingshot from his back pocket. The rooster looked up at him, and immediately decided he had made a mistake. Just as the rooster turned to run, Loran threw the slingshot. It hit him in the back of the head. The rooster keeled over. Loran picked him up and went to the house.

Laying the rooster on the back porch, he entered the house. "Mama, I've killed the flogging rooster."

"What happened? Did he flog you?"

"Yes, and I hit him in the head with my slingshot."

"Get him cleaned while I put a pan of water on to boil. We'll have him for supper."

Loran returned to the porch. The rooster wasn't there. Looking around, he spotted him in the back yard. He was walking around, shaking his head and acting like a drunk person. Loran called into the house. "Don't bother putting water on to boil. I didn't kill him. I only addled him."

That cured the rooster of his flogging. He never again attacked anyone, even children. They could go into his domain and he would turn and go the other way.

About the middle of March that year, it began raining and rained for two weeks. That was usually the time Ben planted the early corn. It would have to wait. Ben fidgeted, but it didn't do any good. The rains kept coming. They started on Wednesday of one week and abruptly stopped on Wednesday two weeks later. The sun came out, and the water-logged soil began the drying out process.

At supper on Friday, Ben said, "I think that upper field will be dry enough to plant tomorrow. We can put our early corn there. Loran, can you help me plant corn tomorrow?"

"I sure can," Loran answered. "What time do you want to start?"

"How about 9:00?"

"Why don't we make it eight?" Loran asked. "We could probably finish by one, and that would give you time for an afternoon nap."

"Okay, we'll start at eight."

The next morning, Ben and Loran had the horses harnessed and ready a little ahead of schedule. They hitched the strongest team to the lister and the spare horse to the planter. Ben started toward the lister. "No," Loran said. "I'm doing the plowing. You can plant."

Ben stopped and looked a little puzzled. "Think you're big enough for the lister?"

"I'm big enough."

Loran plowed one round while Ben watched. Satisfied that Loran could handle the lister, he placed the planter in the first furrow and said, "Giddy-up."

They finished planting that field about 1:00, as scheduled. Ben threw the planter out of gear; Loran laid the lister on its side and they headed for the barn. They put the farm implements away, then un-harnessed the horses and fed and watered them. The team was always taken care of first, before they ate their own meal.

As they entered the house, Tildie asked, "Did you get finished?"

"Yes," Ben answered. "Loran plowed, and he did a good job."

"I told you he would."

Ben had a proud look. "It's hard to realize my little boy is growing up."

"Dinner's ready. As soon as you two get washed up, we can eat."

After they ate, Tildie and Theta began washing the dishes. Ben lay down for his Saturday afternoon nap. Loran left the house to inspect the rest of the fields. The 10-acre plot behind the barn was dry enough to plow. He decided to begin listing it, in preparation for planting hygear. He had almost four hours before time for the evening chores. He could get a lot done in that length of time. Maybe what was lacking, he could finish the next day after church. If that didn't work, he had about two hours after school each day for plowing.

On Sunday, a family of close friends came home from church with Tildie and the children, for Sunday dinner. The plowing would have to wait. That was all right with Loran. Friends and family always came first, and social life was important to the Parker family.

When Loran got home from school on Monday, Ben was still sleeping. His long walk to his ministry engagement on Sunday had taken its toll. Loran hitched one of the horses to the planter and planted what he had listed on Saturday. On Friday after school, Loran finished planting the field of hygear. Ben was surprised and pleased. His little boy had taken the initiative and did part of the planting without his help. There was plenty of planting left to do, but they had a good start.

During that time in Oklahoma, the school year started on the Monday nearest August 15 and ended on the Friday nearest May 15, for a total of 36 weeks. By working during the Easter vacation, Saturday mornings and after school during the week, Ben and Loran had all the crops planted, except cotton, by the end of the school year. They also had the corn and hygear laid by, and had begun the cultivation of the later crops. Ben was pleased. Everything was on schedule. Their watermelon patch was growing nicely, with plenty of immature melons. Their plot of green beans was producing very well. Tildie and Theta were canning them for their winter needs. Tildie's vegetable garden was producing in abundance. They had fresh vegetables every day, and the surplus was canned. It was a happy time for the family.

Cotton is a hot weather plant. It needs hot days and warm nights to set the seedlings and cause the young plants to grow properly. If it's planted too early, the seedlings will just sit there and refuse to grow, even when hot weather does arrive. The mature stalks will be stunted and will produce scant crops. If you've planted too early, you're better off to plow it up and start over. In Oklahoma, cotton was seldom planted before the end of the school year, often later.

That year, hot weather came marching in a few days before school let out for the summer. At supper on Friday, the last day of school, Ben announced, "I think hot weather is here to stay. We probably should plant the cotton tomorrow."

"I'm ready," Loran answered. "If we get an early start, we should be finished by 12:00 or 1:00."

A few minutes after supper, A T stopped for a visit. "I'm going to town tomorrow. Do you need anything? You could ride with me, or I could pick up what you need."

"I need some things from town," Tildie said, "but I need Ben to help me pick them out. Loran, could you work by yourself planting the cotton?"

"Yes, I could," Loran answered.

A T thought for a minute. "Gerald could run the planter for you. I don't have anything important for him to do."

"That would be okay," Loran answered.

James Gerald was A T's oldest son. Although he was only 10 years old, he was large for his age and had already been operating the planter and other light farm implements for A T.

The next morning, A T and Gerald arrived about 8:00. Loran already had the horses harnessed, and was ready to start plowing. He and Gerald went to the field to work and the rest of the family went to town.

Gerald did a good job of keeping up with Loran that morning. When noon arrived, Loran said, "We have about one more hour to finish this field. We have two choices. We can continue working until it's finished, or we can have dinner, then come back for an hour."

"Uncle Loran, I'd just as soon finish first and not have to hitch the horses up for another hour after dinner."

"Okay, that's what we'll do."

Loran and Gerald finished planting the cotton about 1:00 and went to the barn. After feeding and watering the horses, Loran checked the icebox. "No leftovers," he said. "I'll have to cook something for us."

"Can I help?" Gerald asked.

"Yes. Why don't you go to the cellar and pick out two jars of vegetables you like? I'll kill and clean a chicken. We'll have a chicken dinner."

In a few minutes, Loran had chicken frying in the skillet, potatoes boiling in a pot and vegetables heating in other pots. About thirty minutes later, he had a chicken dinner ready. On the menu were fried chicken, mashed potatoes, gravy and two vegetables. Just as they sat down to eat, the rest of the family came through the front door.

"Sit down and eat," Loran said. "There's plenty for everyone."

"My, this is a treat," Tildie said. "I'm not used to getting such a good meal without having to cook it myself."

"Did you finish the planting?" Ben asked.

"Yes, we did. We worked straight through to about 1:00, and got it done."

"That's the last of our planting. All we have to do now is the cultivation."

For the next three years, Loran continued doing most of the farm work. Ben helped out when he could, but he wasn't strong enough to do any of the heavy work. He would operate the planter and the go-devil, but Loran did the more strenuous plowing and cultivating.

Ben continued his circuit ministry in the six churches he served. His family took in stride his Saturday afternoon naps, his Sunday preaching engagements and his Monday resting sessions. Although Ben didn't feel very well most of the time, he was extremely happy to have such an understanding and hard-working family. He considered himself richly blessed.

THE KEROSENE LAMP

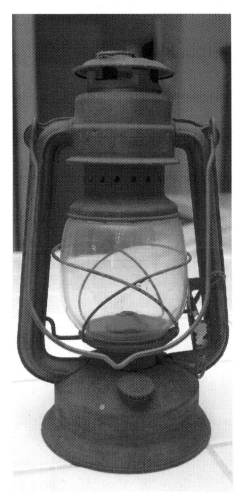

A Kerosene Lamp and a Kerosene Lantern

Ben used a kerosene lamp all his life. It was invented and in use long before his birth in 1886. It continued as the most-used light source for the farming community until after his death in 1948. Other light sources were developed during the early 1900s: the gas lamp and the electric light. Even so, the rural communities, with no electric lines or gas pipes, still used the kerosene lamp. During his entire farming career, Ben always owned at least one of each type of kerosene light: the lamp for indoor use and the lantern for outdoor use.

The design for the kerosene lamp was first described by al-Razi, in ninth century Baghdad, in his *Book of Secrets.* A more modern version was constructed by the Polish inventor, Ignacy Lukasiewicz in 1853. Lukasiewicz's invention was timely. In 1847, a young Scotsman by the name of James Young developed the process of making kerosene. Later, in 1849, Abraham Gesner devised a method to distill kerosene from petroleum.

These developments made kerosene readily available by the time of Lukasiewicz's invention, and put an end to the whaling industry. The price of sperm oil couldn't compete with the price of kerosene, which was 59 cents a gallon in 1865, and had dropped to just over seven cents a gallon by 1895.

The kerosene lamp gained international notoriety with the Great Chicago Fire, which began burning about 9:00 p.m. on Sunday, October 8, 1871. The fire started in or close to a barn owned by Patrick and Catherine (Kate) O'Leary. Even though Kate insisted she was in bed early that evening, her neighbors claimed her cow kicked over a kerosene lamp and started the fire. Although later evidence exonerated her, the legend still persists.

Two versions of the kerosene lamp were in popular use: the wick lamp and the pressure lamp. The pressure lamp was brighter, but it had a number of working parts which could, and often did, fail. The wick lamp was the one most farmers used. It is still used in third-world countries, and sometimes used in the United States for emergency lighting when electrical blackouts occur.

The wick lamp has a small fuel tank at the bottom, called the font. A wick, usually made of cotton, is inserted into the font and protrudes out the top through an opening. The opening contains an adjusting mechanism, consisting of an adjusting knob which rotates a small sprocket wheel, known as a cric. The cric raises or lowers the wick. Surrounding the top of the wick, there is a flame protector. It is hinged to allow it to be folded out of the way, to trim the wick. Above the tank is a glass globe which has three functions: It protects the flame from sudden, strong air currents; it draws fresh air from beneath for a brighter flame; and it keeps the flame from being an excessive fire hazard.

Kerosene lamps work on much the same principle as a candle. Capillary action brings kerosene to the top of the wick. As the flame burns the kerosene away, more is osmosed to the top, to replace what has been consumed.

Most kerosene lamps used in the home were made of glass, except for the adjusting mechanism and the globe holders, which were made of metal, and could easily be replaced when they became rusted or corroded. Handled with care, glass lamps would last a lifetime, whereas ones made of metal would begin corroding after a few years. Kerosene lanterns, on the other hand, were made of metal. Glass lamps were not conducive to being carried outdoors, and would tip over easier than lanterns.

The kerosene lamp was one of the most useful inventions of all times. It was in constant use, with practically no changes, for a full century.

Ben cared for his kerosene lamps much the same way he cared for his family: with loving care and finesse. He knew how to keep them in good working order. The font had to be properly filled. If the kerosene became too low, the flame would not be very bright. The wick had to be kept properly trimmed. It also had to be at the proper height. If the wick was too low, the flame would be small and not very bright. Too high, and it would smoke, giving off soot made up of unburned kerosene, blacking the globe and reducing the amount of light which could penetrate it.

To trim the wick, Ben placed the lamp on a flat surface, flipped the flame guard out of the way, and used a pair of scissors to cut the burnt part off. He was careful to cut it parallel to the surface the lamp sat on. After trimming the wick, he snipped a small amount off each corner, so the flame would not peak at its extremities, thus causing it to smoke at the outer edges. Ben taught all his children the fine art of caring for a kerosene lamp.

A kerosene lamp was used for almost all the Parkers' lighting needs. Ben's family used one while eating supper. After the meal, dishes were washed by the light of a kerosene lamp. After those chores were done, the family gathered around one or more lamps to do homework for school, do Bible study, or to read. Ben studied for many sermons by the light of a kerosene lamp. In doing so, he instilled study habits in his children that served them well in school.

During the school year of 1947 and 1948, Loran put one of the Parkers' kerosene lamps to good use. His high school English teacher, Mrs. Beth Beavers, was stressing literature that year, and he became enamored with reading. He did his homework during the period each subject was taught. Then, during study hall, the last period of the day, he would check out a library book and begin reading. He continued reading on his one-hour bus ride home. After chores and supper were done, he returned to his book and read by the light of a kerosene lamp until the book was finished, usually between 10:00 and 11:00 at night. That year, he read every Zane Gray and Jack London book in his school library, along with many other authors. By the end of the year, he had turned in 37 book reports.

Ben was extremely gratified with the accomplishments of his young son, both on the farm and in school.

YEAR OF REST

An Old Barn
This barn has vertical-board construction, similar to the ones Ben used.

In December of 1946, Ben's health rapidly deteriorated. By January, he could no longer do any work. Walking just a few feet caused shortness of breath and exhaustion. He was forced to cancel all his circuit preaching engagements. He didn't want to, but it was impossible to walk to them or exert any energy preaching. He spent many hours each day sitting in his comfortable chair, sleeping most of the time. His doctor said his condition was caused by his heart illness. Perhaps he had congestive heart failure. The symptoms were all there, but the diagnostic abilities of the doctors of that time were not sufficiently advanced to tell if that was the case. Congestive heart failure was not positively diagnosed until a much later date. At the time, it was just a part of heart disease.

About the middle of December of that year, Ben and Loran were talking during supper. "You will need to do all the farm work now," Ben said.

"I had already decided that," Loran answered. "I can tell you aren't able to do any work."

"I'll help you all I can."

"You don't need to do anything. Just rest. That's the best thing you can do for me."

Ben was in deep thought for a few minutes. "Since you will be doing all the work, I guess that means you will be making the decisions. It's your farming operation now."

"I'm prepared to do that. I'm 16 and have done everything there is to do concerning farming. I'm ready to make the decisions."

In order to accomplish what he needed to do, Loran worked after school, on Saturdays and during vacation times. Tildie helped with the chores, such as feeding the chickens and livestock, milking the cows and gathering eggs. Theta did most of the cooking and housecleaning when she wasn't in school.

Loran could sense that his papa wouldn't last much longer, so he began asking questions about their ancestry. Ben hadn't talked much about them, due to the incident with Lilla in his early years.

"Are we kin to the outlaw Bonnie Parker?" Loran asked.

"Yes, we are," Ben answered. "I'm not sure just where she fits in. Your brother, Francis, has read a diary that Poppa had before he died. He read it twice, and I read it when I was a child. It is about two Parker brothers who came to America from England in the early 1600s. We are descendents of one of those brothers, but I don't know which. Bonnie is also a descendent of one of them. I don't know if the connection is through Elder John Parker or goes back all the way to England. Either way, we're kin to her."

"Can you give me the names of some of our ancestors?"

"Sure. Of course you know my father's name is Benjamin Franklin (Doc) Parker. My grandpa is Edward Marion Parker. My great grandpa is Steven W. Parker. My great-great grandpa is Daniel Parker. From there, everything becomes fuzzy. Elder John had a son named Daniel, but I don't know if he's our ancestor or another Daniel from the other Parker line."

"Thank you, Papa. At least I have some names now."

As the winter wore on and spring arrived, Ben's condition slowly worsened. He did little walking, except to go to the table for his meals. He didn't want to become such a burden as to be served his meals in bed. Even though he couldn't do any work, he didn't want to cause extra effort for the rest of the family. Although Tildie would gladly have fed him in bed, she respected his wishes and allowed him to come to the table to eat. She didn't want to deprive him of his pride.

In early March, Ben and Loran were talking at suppertime. "Are you going to plant some cotton?" Ben asked.

"No," Loran responded.

"Then, what are you going to do for a cash crop?"

"Papa, I've seen you borrow money for cotton seed year after year and have the boll weevils get most of the crop. You seldom made enough from it to pay off the note. I have enough money for corn and hygear seed. I'd have to borrow money to plant cotton. I'll plant the entire farm in corn and hygear, to feed the livestock. I'll work for the extra money we need."

"Okay. You're in charge. Do what you think is best."

About the middle of March, Loran began planting the early corn. Since he was still in school, he worked after school and Saturdays. He would finish it during Easter vacation. Spring break came early that year. Saturday, March 29, began Easter week.

While Loran was planting the early corn, holes appeared in the soles of his work shoes. To make them last as long as possible, he began cutting cardboard to fit the inside of his shoes. It would last for about four hours before a hole appeared in the cardboard. He would place his homemade inner soles in each shoe in the morning, and again when he went back to work in the afternoon. He didn't have any money for new shoes, and he was determined to plant that year's crop without having to borrow any money.

On Wednesday of that week, Roden came by their house on the way to Lindsay. Loran was in the fields plowing. "Loran is working in worn-out shoes," Tildie said. "He has a large hole in the sole of each shoe."

"That's not good," Roden answered. "Can you have him come to the house?"

Tildie went to the field where Loran was plowing and motioned for him to come to her. He stopped the horses and came to where she was. "Roden wants to talk to you."

"Okay," he said. "I'll leave the team where it is. I'll be back as soon as I talk to Roden."

Roden said, "Let me see your shoes."

Loran took one shoe off and handed it to him. The sole contained a large hole. The cardboard inner sole was almost worn through. "You need to come to town with me and let me get you a new pair of work shoes."

"I don't have time. I need to get that field plowed by dark. I have lots of plowing and planting to do and not much time to do it."

Roden looked stern. "All you have to do is step on a sharp stick and you won't be doing any plowing for several weeks. That will put you behind more than going to town with me."

"I don't have any money for new shoes."

"You don't need any money. I'll buy them."

Loran thought for a few seconds. "You're right. A sharp stick would put me out of commission. But, I don't know when I could pay you back."

"You don't need to pay me back. I know you are trying to get this crop planted without borrowing any money. I admire you for that. But, I'm doing this as much for Papa as for you. He's depending on you to get this crop planted."

"Okay," Loran answered. "Just let me put the plow away and unharness the team."

In a few hours, Roden and Loran returned from town. Loran had a new pair of work shoes. He thanked his brother profusely and prepared to return to the fields. He wouldn't have to bother with cutting inner soles for his shoes any more.

Loran finished the early corn planting during that Easter vacation. On Monday, April 7, he returned to school with no looming deadlines hanging over his head. It would be a relatively easy task to do the cultivation after school each day. He was pleased with the progress he had made.

Not long after Easter, Loran heard rumors that the Butler Grocery in Lindsay, a small mom and pop store, needed a helper on Saturdays. He applied for the job and was hired. From then until broomcorn season, he worked every Saturday. He rode his bicycle the ten miles to town, worked all day, then rode it back home. That job helped supply some much needed money to buy basic groceries and supplies for the family.

Broomcorn cutting started about the middle of June and lasted until about the first of August. As in previous years, Loran was hired as a part of Fred Baker's crew. He cut broomcorn almost every day during that season. That year, he earned $1.25 per hour, good part-time wages for the era. The money earned would have to supply the family with necessities until the next season.

Broomcorn cutting is hard, hot work. The seeds have a fuzzy material that will cause stinging and itching on the tender parts of one's skin. As a result, those cutting it needed to wear long-sleeve shirts, a good hat and a bandana around their neck. Working in the hot, humid sunshine of Oklahoma and wearing clothing like that caused one to perspire profusely. That, along with the stinging and itching fuzz, caused Loran to have to take a bath every night. Tildie, Theta and Loran devised a plan. Loran built a small, wooden platform behind the house. On it, he placed a number three washtub. Each afternoon, Theta would draw enough water from the well to fill it about one-third full. Sitting in the Oklahoma sun, it would warm to bath temperature before dark. Just before the light faded, Theta would place clean clothes on the platform for Loran. Since Loran always came home after dark from broomcorn cutting, he could bathe in the ambient light from the window, put on clean clothes and place the fuzz-filled ones in the clothes hamper. Since he was behind the house, he couldn't be seen from the road.

One afternoon, Theta forgot about drawing water for Loran's bath. It was almost dark by the time she thought of it. In that part of the country, well water always came out cold. Loran didn't have a warm bath that night; he had a cold one. Theta felt bad about that, and never again forgot to draw his bath water on time.

By the time broomcorn season was over, it was almost time to begin the next school term. Loran used those few days to gather part of the crops he had planted that spring. The rest of them were gathered after school and on Saturdays. By the middle of October, all the crops were in the barn.

One afternoon, a few days after the last of the crops were gathered, Ben walked to the barn. His steps were slow and faltering and he had to stop often to rest. It took him 30 minutes to make the 200-foot trek from the house to the barn. Ordinarily, he would walk two miles in that length of time.

When Ben got there, he opened the door. What he saw both surprised and pleased him. It was stacked to the rafters with bundles of hygear. Walking around the barn, he checked the corncrib. It was filled to the brim with nice, large ears of corn. *The livestock will have plenty to eat this winter*, he thought. Closing the crib door, he returned to the house.

That night at supper, Ben said, "Loran, I checked the barn this afternoon. You did a good job with the farm this year. I'm proud of you."

"Thank you," Loran answered.

"How about your money? Do you have enough to last until next summer?"

"I turned the money over to Mama. She can manage it better than I can. How about it, Mama? Do we have enough to last until next summer?"

"Unless we have a big, unforeseen expense, we have more than enough," Tildie answered.

"You've proved yourself this year," Ben said. "I won't have to worry about you anymore. You'll make it just fine."

The trip to the barn was hard on Ben, but he just had to know for sure his family wouldn't suffer because of his illness. He spent most of the time during the next few days just sitting in his chair and sleeping. But, it was worth it. A heavy load had been lifted. He had no more worries about his family's welfare.

On Sunday, January 25, 1948, Ben's condition became worse. He was almost in a coma and could not get off the bed. He slept most of the time. About the only time he was awake was at meal times, to eat a small amount of food for nourishment. Tildie fed him his meals at his bedside.

On Tuesday morning of that week, Loran could tell that his papa was near death. "Do I need to stay home today?" he asked.

"No," Tildie answered. "Your papa wants you to get the best education you can. He wouldn't approve of your staying home."

At noon that day, Tildie fed Ben his dinner, then had her own meal. After she ate, she did the dishes. Returning to Ben's bedside, she was surprised to find him wide awake and obviously wanting to talk.

"What did I do to deserve such a good wife and family?" he asked.

"You're a good man, Ben. You've worked hard all your life to be sure all of us had what we needed. You deserve no less than a good family."

"But, I feel so useless right now," Ben answered. "I can't work and Loran is having to take my place."

"In addition to our family, just think of all the people you've helped. You are not useless. You've led a fulfilled life."

"That's true. I guess I was just feeling sorry for myself. But, I did want you to know that I love you."

"I love you, too," Tildie answered. "I've loved you since the time we first met in Brock. You have been the only man in my life."

"There's not anything I can do now to help our family. It's up to you and the children now."

"You look tired," Tildie said. "Why don't you get some sleep?"

After their conversation, Ben slipped into a coma. About ten minutes later, he gasped and drew his last breath.

COME HOME, MY CHILD

Gladys Lavada Parker
In this picture, Lavada was 12 years old, about one year before her death.

January twenty-seven,
Nineteen forty-eight,
   The last circuit preacher
Saw the golden gate.

   In that fair land,
Which needs no sun,
   God welcomed him,
And said, "Well done."

   And standing near
The gates of pearl,
   He once again
Saw his little girl.
     (L H P)

Throughout the last year of Ben's extreme illness, during the time he was too weak to do any work, a dramatic and significant change took place. Most folks in rural societies had acquired automobiles and began driving into the surrounding towns to attend larger churches. Diminutive urban congregations, which were meeting in local schoolhouses, quickly faded away. Small, country one and two-room school districts were absorbed into city schools and their accompanying halls of learning rotted, collapsed and returned to dust. Most rural churches suffered the same fate.

On a Tuesday afternoon, God's last circuit preacher left this world behind. The moment Ben went home to be with his Lord and his little darling, the need for a circuit preacher died with him.

God's timing is always perfect.

ABOUT THE AUTHOR

Loran Hugh Parker was born on September 28, 1930, three miles south of Bradley, Oklahoma; about 60 miles south of Oklahoma City. Having begun the primary grade at the Oak Grove School, Loran spent all except three months of his nine elementary school years at a small, country, two-room school named Pikes Peak, in south-central Oklahoma. It was located ten miles southwest of Lindsay, Oklahoma. He graduated from high school at a small oil town, now gone, called Cox City, Oklahoma, not far from the Pikes Peak School District. He spent two years at the East Central State Teacher's College, now East Central University, in eastern Oklahoma, located at Ada. During his second year at East Central, he married Beverly June Stafford of Porterville, California, and at the end of the term, they moved to California.

Loran graduated from Fresno State College, now University of California Fresno, in June, 1962, with a major in Mathematics and a minor in Physical/Life Science. He obtained a teaching credential the next year and began his career in teaching. He taught math for 30 years, with a few classes in science, photography and art. He retired from public school teaching in June, 1990, but continued part-time at West Coast Christian College for one more year.

Loran has always loved writing, and began writing poetry at age ten. He has also enjoyed telling stories of his youth to his children and grandchildren. He self-published a memoirs book titled <u>I Love Papa's Stories</u> in the spring of 2008. He has also had technical math articles, stories, and poems published in various books and magazines. When curriculum was not available in any area of math, he wrote it himself. He was on writing teams for the Fresno Unified School District, producing math curriculum for underachievers.

Since January, 2005, Loran has been taking writing classes, taught by Janice Stevens, at Clovis Adult Education. He is now in the process of writing his second memoirs book.